Children & The Law

Children & The Law

A Series of Conference Papers
presented at
De Montfort University, Leicester
October 1993

Edited by

Deborah J Lockton LLB MPhil

De Montfort University, Leicester

De Montfort University Law Monographs
Cavendish Publishing Limited

First published in Great Britain 1994 by Cavendish Publishing Limited,
The Glass House, Wharton Street, London WC1X 9PX
Telephone: 071-278 8000   Facsimile: 071 278 8080

British Library Cataloguing in Publication Data

Lockton, Deborah J
Children & the Law
I Title
344.20287

ISBN 1 85941 111 8
Printed and bound in Great Britain

The Contributors

Professor Judith Masson is Professor of Law at the University of Warwick.

Penny Booth is a Senior Lecturer in Law at the University of Teesside.

Roger Cockfield is a Reader in Taxation at De Montfort University, Leicester.

Mary Mulholland is a Senior Lecturer in Law at De Montfort University, Leicester.

Maria Ruegger is a Senior Lecturer in Applied Social Sciences, Bedford College of Higher Education, and Guardian Ad Litem, Hertfordshire Panel.

Linda Delany is a Senior Lecturer in Law at Manchester Metropolitan University.

Dr Christine Piper is Joint Director of the Centre for the Study of Law, the Child and the Family, at Brunel University.

Felicity Kaganas is Associate Director of the Centre for the Study of Law, the Child and the Family at Brunel University.

Ian Mallinson is Director of Social Work, Moray House Institute, Heriot Watt University, Edinburgh, and Vice-Chairperson of the Social Care Association's Social Care Practice Committee.

Lindsey Mendoza is an Associate Senior Lecturer in Law at Anglia Polytechnic University.

Margaret Ford is a Senior Lecturer in Law at the Bolton Institute of Higher Education.

Nell Wood is a Principal Officer, Social Services Department, Registration and Inspection Unit, Bolton Metropolitan Borough.

Introduction

This monograph is a series of papers presented at a conference held at De Montfort University, Leicester in October 1993, to discuss the changes in relation to the law relating to children over recent years. The conference sought to bring together both academics and practitioners from law, social work and other related disciplines to discuss and debate legal issues relating to children and the monograph reflects this diversity of approach. The keynote paper is by Professor Judith Masson, who addresses the issues of young persons and the rights to independence under the Children Act 1989. The next two papers look at the Child Support Act 1991. Penny Booth discusses the broader implications of the Act for children and their families; Roger Cockfield and Mary Mullholland look at the taxation implications of the legislation. The following two papers look at children and consent to medical treatment. Maria Ruegger analyses the recent cases on withholding and giving of medical consent where the child is 'Gillick competent' and Linda Delany looks at the interesting area of parents consenting on behalf of a child for non-therapeutic medical treatment, for example bone marrow donation, and the legal dilemmas which may arise.

The final three papers deal with aspects of the Children Act 1989. Felicity Kaganas and Christine Piper look at joint parenting under the Act, Ian Mallinson investigates the problems in the legal duties to provide day care for under school age children and Lindsey Mendoza looks at the use of prohibited steps orders and the protection of children. A further paper is reproduced which was distributed at the conference by Margaret Ford and Nell Wood. This is an analysis of the implementation of the requirements under the Children Act to provide day care services.

Deborah J Lockton

Contents

Table of Cases

Table of Statutes

Chapter 1

The Children Act 1989 and Young People: Dependence and Rights to Independence

Professor Judith Masson
Warwick University

The aim of this paper is to explore the impact of the Children Act 1989 and other recent social legislation on the competing portrayals of children as dependants of their families and independent decision-makers. It focuses on adolescents, particularly young people between the ages of 16 and 18. This age group has been the target of changes in benefit legislation in order to further the family and economic policies of the Conservative Government and has also had to bear the brunt of changes in the employment markets in the 1980s. These changes have produced a new dependency, an extended childhood of older children and young adults. The state does not wish to take responsibility for these young people but wants them to remain within their families. Consequently, this new dependency, unlike the dependency of young children (and of wives), is not being reflected in protective legislation. Rather, dependency may be used as a justification for denying rights. This is seen most clearly in the House of Lords cases of *R v LB Tower Hamlets ex p Begum* and *R v LB Bexley ex p B* (1993)[1] where it was accepted that a mentally infirm woman of 23 could not be an applicant for housing because she was dependent on her family. Similar reasoning precluded applications for housing by young children. Thus parents who had been found intentionally homeless could not avoid the consequence of disqualification from rehousing under Part III of the Housing Act 1985 and this disqualification affected their children.

The Children Act 1989 says comparatively little about people aged 16-18. These young people have been recognised because of maturity or age-specific legislation, as having the capacity to make most decisions about their own lives. This new independence conflicts with the new dependency to produce a confused framework for the transition from child to adult.

Context of the Children Act

The context of the Children Act 1989 is usually discussed in terms of the need for coherent law reform (DHSS 1985; Law Commission 1988) and a

---

1   (1993) 25 HLR 319.

re–orienting of the state's approach to child protection following a series of child death enquiry reports and the crisis in Cleveland (Bainham 1990 p 3; Fox-Harding 1991 p 180). Such a discussion highlights issues of state intervention, and the problem that state action may undermine family life by action which pays inadequate attention to parent/child relationships, and the importance of those relationships to children's well-being, but make obscure consideration of the separate relationship between the child and the welfare state.

There is, however, an alternative context which places the Act within the agenda of the New Right. This focuses attention on the issue of the family's responsibility for its members, and the need to reduce state involvement in domestic and commercial life.

Young people were targeted throughout the 1980s in furtherance of this agenda (Jones and Wallace 1992 p 60) with a reduction and later a withdrawal of social security benefits (Social Security Acts 1980-1988), requirements to attend schemes in order to qualify for any state financial support and removal of the protection of Wages Councils which set minimum levels of pay (Wages Act 1986). Young people were effectively forced to continue the financial dependency on their families because other sources of income through employment or state benefits were not open to them. Dependency was maintained by making it more difficult for young people to separate from their families through restrictions on payments for board and lodging accommodation and the lack of availability of affordable rented accommodation for people of any age. These changes were presented as ending the state's attack on the family. However, they sought to impose a particular (middle class) approach to the period of transition from childhood to adulthood (Harris 1989 p 110) which had the advantage of reducing state expenditure.

This extension of childhood was also predicated on the existence of a family (or at least one adult) who was able and willing to support the young person; where the adult was in receipt of benefits the expectation of support was reversed so that benefits were reduced on the basis that the young person was contributing to the expenses of the household despite their inevitably meagre income (Harris 1989 pp 72-3). Although there is evidence of mutual obligations within families (Finch 1989) these rules did not reflect what was happening in the families affected by them, but what ought to happen irrespective of personal circumstances. In this context young people are soft targets for the withdrawal of state support because they are not full citizens and because the notion of the strong family is one which, at the level of rhetoric, draws widespread support.

Withdrawal of state benefits did not lead to a massive reduction of state expenditure in social security, rather it allowed some containment of benefit costs despite a gradual growth in the number of people over pensionable age and a massive increase in the long term unemployed created in two recessions and the 'restructuring' of industry. In effect young people (and their families) were required to pay for these changes, both financially and by the reduction of choice that dependence produces for both parties.

Aims of the Children Act 1989

Just as the context of the Children Act can be viewed in a number of ways so too can its aims. The Act sought to make a number of shifts in relationships between families, children and the state, between social services departments and other local authority departments, voluntary organisations and the state, and between the courts, families and local authorities. The aims of the legislation may be identified through a study of the preparatory material, particularly the white paper - The law on child care and family services (1987), parliamentary debates, material prepared for the implementation programme (Masson 1992) and subsequent academic analyses. From these emerge three predominal themes: balance; parental responsibility and welfare.

Balance

The White Paper recognised that there was a need to establish 'a better balance' (CM 62 1987 para 9) between the state, individual parents and children. It portrayed the state's role as pivotal so that a shift towards the interests of parents could be viewed as operating to the detriment of children but noted that recognising parent's interests could be of benefit to children. A better balance would be established by controlling state intervention (for example by reducing the duration of, and allowing parental challenge to a place of safety order), providing state support for families to avoid the need for compulsory action and emphasising the value of continuing parental involvement if parents and children had to separate. Academics have also recognised the attempt to balance competing interests in child care policy within the Children Act. Fox-Harding has identified four distinct streams: laissez-faire/patriarchy, state paternalism, defence of the birth family and children's rights which are all reflected in the Act but notes that the use of the term 'balance' denies the conflict and dilemmas which the field of state/family relations inevitably causes (Fox-Harding 1991 p 231). The idea of balance is also problematic when the reduction of influence on one or more player is not matched by increase of power for the others. Parental responsibility for adolescents is declining as their capacity to make decisions is reflected in rights to do so. However, young people's opportunities to live independent of their parents are restricted by their financial dependency on them. The state opting out of any role which might transfer dependency to it leaves a vacuum where young people are viewed both as independent and dependent according to the issue under discussion, but neither they nor their parents are able to avoid the conflict of status which results.

Parental responsibility

John Eekelaar has identified two ideas behind the concept of parental responsibility - that parents must behave dutifully towards their children and that responsibility belongs to the parents not the state (Eekelaar 1991 p 39). He argues that the second idea replaced the first as the dominant conception with the belief that reduction of supervision or control would encourage parents to behave more responsibly towards their children (p 49). Eekelaar questions the basis for such a view noting that a similar approach was not taken to the regulation of care outside the family. A further point arises in relation to adolescents - what is the nature of parental responsibility to them? If parents have come to expect that childhood ends at 16 (or 18), what legal principles ensure that ties of kinship are recognised as imposing duties and responsibilities beyond that age?

Removing state power does not necessarily change the climate for family responsibility particularly where elements of the old order remain. The fact that parental responsibility is both a private law and public law concept containing powers derived from the common law and from statute means that legislating for a new notion of parental responsibility without clearly identifying its new contents is problematic. Removing benefits from 16-18 year olds may be viewed as placing responsibility for their care on the families but does not do so whilst parents may cease to be liable to support their children when they reach age 16.[2]

Welfare

Welfare had to be central to the Children Act 1989 because of its established position (any move away from the paramountcy principle could be viewed as reducing the importance of children's well-being) and the lack of any alternative framework for the wide range of disputes about children which could be brought before the courts. Welfare is a problematic concept because it allows wide discretion to decision-makers and the favouring of particular values. The addition of the check-list does not solve these but may help avoid decision error by acting as an aide-memoire. Also it may assist advisers to explain to clients what the relevant issues are for the court (Law Commission

---

2   The Provisions are extremely complex and do not provide a coherent system. If a child is looked after by the local authority parents cease to be liable to contribute to this when the child reaches 16 (Children Act 1989 Schedule 2 para 21(3)(a)). Under the Child Support Act 1991, s 55 an 'absent parent' owes a duty to support a 'qualifying' child. This includes a child in full time education up to the age of 19 and all children up to the age of 16. There is provision for regulations to designate other cases where the child is under 18. Where a child or young person is supported by Income Support parents are liable relatives. In some cases this liability continues to the age of 19 where the child/young person is not in full-time education their restricted access to benefits means that their parent cannot be liable to the state, see Income Support (General) Regulations 1987 and Social Security Administration Act 1992.

1988 para 3.18). Despite the wording of s 1(1) the emphasis given to welfare may have been reduced because of the so-called non-intervention principle (Bainham 1990 p 209). This was certainly intended to discourage recourse to the courts and the making of court orders (Law Commission 1988). The removal of the court's duty to approve on welfare grounds the arrangements in all cases of divorce also provides a further example of the rolling back of the state. The welfare check-list includes: 'a) the ascertainable wishes and feelings of the child concerned considered in the light of his age and understanding)' and thus it seems possible for the concept of welfare to contain both adult views and those of the young person. The balance between these elements is a matter for the individual judge but it has been suggested by Lord Donaldson that 'good parenting involves giving minors as much rope as they can possible handle without an unacceptable risk that they will hang themselves' (*Re W (A minor) (Medical Treatment)* (1992)).[3]

However, welfare decision-making about young people by the courts is also limited by the restricted jurisdiction in relation to the over 16s. Section 8 orders can only be made in exceptional circumstances (s 9(7)), reflecting the notion that parental responsibility has effectively ended when children reach this age. The inherent jurisdiction remains available because the High Court has claimed powers which go beyond parental responsibility (*Re R (A Minor) (Wardship: Medical Treatment)* (1991))[4]. However, medical decisions about over 16-year-old children have also been justified on the basis of statutory provisions extending parental power. It is possible, therefore, that the exceptional circumstances provision could be interpreted to allow prohibited steps and specific issue orders where it is clear from statute that parental power still exists.[5]

The emphasis on welfare was also reduced within the public sector by changing the nature of the local authority's duty from a requirement to give first consideration to the welfare of the children in care (Child Care Act 1980 s 18) which had been interpreted as potentially demanding priority for children over other client groups (*Liddle v Sunderland BC* (1983)).[6] Local authorities are now only required to 'safeguard and promote' the welfare of children they are looking after (Children Act 1989 s 22(3)) and to advise, assist and befriend them 'with a view to promoting' their welfare when they cease to be looked after.

---

3   [1992] 4 All ER 627 at 638..

4   [1991] 4 All ER 177 at 186; [1992] 1 FLR 190 at 199.

5   Where a young person wishes to marry but a parent refuses to consent the courts have jurisdiction to grant permission (Marriage Act 1949 s 3). If marriage is viewed as part of upbringing the welfare test applies but most of these cases take place in the magistrates' courts and are not reported so it is impossible to know what is considered (Cretney and Masson 1990 p 9).

6   [1983] 13 Fam Law 252-3.

Children's rights

The Child Care Law Review referred to children's rights as a 'slogan in search of a definition'[7] but was able to discern two distinct and often competing aspects - rights to be provided with the means to take their place in adult society, and rights of self-determination. John Eekelaar categorised these as emerging from 'developmental' and 'autonomy' interests (Eekelaar 1986 p 171). These could give rise to children's rights on the basis that they might conceivably be claimed (in retrospect) by children for themselves, rather than merely asserted by adults in furtherance of their own interests.

Eekelaar's developmental interest requires that resources are allocated 'so that an individual child does not suffer such deprivations during childhood that he is disadvantaged disproportionately when compared to children generally' (p 172). It therefore depends on public and political support and may become enmeshed in wider considerations of public policy. The UN Convention on Rights of the Child (UN 1989) requires States Parties to recognise the rights of disabled children to special care which will facilitate the child's active participation in the community (Art 23(1)) and the rights of all children to the highest attainable standard of health care (Art 24(1)). Although social measures are limited by the extent of available resources (Art 4) adopting the Convention appears to require an acceptance that health provision for children should be at least as good as that provided for adults. This might justify a broader definition of the developmental interest which would allow comparisons not just with other children but with adults.

At first sight the Children Act seems to recognise the developmental interest through the provision for 'children in need'. Local authorities have a general duty to provide a range in level of service to meet the requirements of children in need (s 17). Although individual children (or their families) seem to have no rights to any particular service they may complain about services provided or refused and may seek judicial review of decisions which are illegal, unreasonable, or procedurally improper (Sunkin 1992 p 101). The Children Act 1989 can be regarded as providing the framework for community care for children and young people who are consequently not within the community care duties under the NHS and Community Care Act 1990. However, there is a major distinction between the construction of the local authority's duty under these Acts. The 1990 Act explicitly provides a duty to assess need (s 47(1)(a)) and thus separates the decision about need from that of available resources. Assessment and recording of need facilitates the future development of services, if this occurs for adult services and not for children there is a danger that resources will be skewed to the adult population whose need appears greater. Assessment is also a service in its own right

---

7   DHSS 1985 para 2.16.

(DH 1990, para 3.15). Parents who are well informed about their children's needs may seek to meet them in other ways than by recourse to social services. In practice there may be little distinction because authorities seek to avoid assessment where the applicant is likely not to meet eligibility criteria for rationed services (Health and Social Services Committee 1992-3) although this is open to challenge. The distinction cannot be justified by reference to the need to maintain an appropriate balance between the state and the family because the duty to assess is a service of support rather than a process of intervention. Families cannot be required to submit to a needs assessment, not to accept services which are considered appropriate. Rather it seems to reflect a lower priority to the young.

Eekelaar recognises that the autonomy interest may conflict with the child's basic and developmental interests and suggests that it may conflict with the child's basic and developmental interests and suggests that it may be subordinate to them (p 171). He notes that Lord Scarman's reasoning in *Gillick* establishes the primacy of the child's decision even where adults consider that the decision does not accord with the child's best interests (p 181). Where young people remain at home, dependent on their families, the social policy of maintaining family support for them may also conflict with the independence that the autonomy right provides. It may therefore be necessary to give recognition to parents' views. There is some indication that both Lords Scarman and Fraser recognised this in the *Gillick* case. Lord Scarman indicated that the capacity to make decisions involved a high level of understanding of a broad range of issues which went beyond the child's health to 'moral and family questions', especially her relationship with her parents (*Gillick v West Norfolk and Wisbech Area Health Authority* (1985)[8]). Lord Fraser considered that treatment for a child under 16 should only be given without involvement of the parents in exceptional cases (p 413). Both Law Lords emphasised the importance of adapting the common law to fit with social conditions and might have given less weight to the emotional capacity of teenagers had the decision arisen now when most teenagers remain dependent on their families, at least until the age of majority.

The Children Act and young people's rights

To Social Services

The Lord Chancellor, introducing the Children Bill to the Lords stated that it 'did nothing to alter the underlying principle of *Gillick*'.[9] The impact of

---

8   [1985] 3 All ER 402, 424.
9   Hansard, Lords Vol 502 Col 1351.

Gillick is clear in the statutory provisions relating to assessments which recognise the integrity of mature children, even though a refusal could preclude any protective action. But the power to override a mature child's refusal has now been claimed by the High Court (*Re W (A Minor) (Medical Treatment)* (1992)[10]). However, a closer analysis of the Act shows that it has removed rights which mature minors had previously and failed to make clear where they could act independently. For example, children under 16 can no longer enter and remain in local authority accommodation without parental permission (s 20(7)(8)(11)). The Act is silent about the right of access of under 16s to other part III services but children and young people can only be offered advice confidentially because assistance must be subject to a means test of the parents (s 17(8)).

In legal proceedings

Care proceedings are rarely brought in relation to older teenagers although there is power to make care and supervision orders in respect of under 17s who are not married (s 31(3)). The inherent jurisdiction may be used by local authorities in relation to anyone under 18 with leave but can no longer lead to committal to care nor supervision (s 100(2)). Protection for young people would generally occur through providing them with support to separate from the harm, but control could be exercised through the High Court (*Re W (A Minor) (Medical Treatment)* (1992)),[11] under the Mental Health Act 1983 or through the criminal law.

In care proceedings the child or young person is normally represented by a guardian *ad litem* and a solicitor. The child may not dismiss the guardian *ad litem* but can instruct the solicitor if he or she has the understanding to do so and may terminate the solicitor's appointment (Family Proceedings Courts (Children Act 1989) Rules 1991, r 12(1)(a)(3)). Under the inherent jurisdiction the child is normally but not necessarily a party (Masson and Morton 1989 p 728; Hunt 1993 p 27). Where children are parties they may act without next friend only if the court accepts the solicitor's judgment that they are able to do so.[12] There is some support for older teenagers acting independently (*Re H (Minors)*).[13] Where the child acts without next friend the court may still involve the Official Solicitor as *amicus curiae* and subject the child to his approach (Masson 1992). Even though children may be accepted as having the capacity to give instructions in care or related proceedings they have no right to attend if they are represented by a solicitor (s 95; Family

---

10   [1992] 4 All ER 627.

11   [1992] 4 All ER 627.

12   Family Proceedings Rules 1991 r 9.2A; *Re CT (A Minor) (Wardship: Representation)* [1993] 2 FLR 278.

13   Unreported 6 August 1992.

Proceedings Courts (Children Act Rules) 1991, r 16(2)). There must however, be some doubt whether proceedings can be conducted fairly in the absence of a party who wishes to give instructions to their representative. The High Court which has traditionally conducted proceedings in the absence of the child, taking a paternalistic view of the effects, seems reluctant to accept that they should have a right to attend (*Re C (A Minor) (Care: Child's Wishes)*[14]).

In private law proceedings the leave requirement provides a hurdle that only mature children can cross (s 10(8)). The height of the hurdle is set by the court by determining what must be understood and at what level. The Practice Direction,[15] requiring such cases to be transferred to the High Court would seem to raise the hurdle although the Court of Appeal has made it clear that wardship cannot be used to impose a guardian *ad litem* in private law cases (*Re CT (A Minor) (Wardship: Representation)* (1993)).[16] Few applications are likely to be made by older teenagers because of the restriction of s 8 orders to exceptional cases. Section 8 orders, with the exception of contact orders relate to issues of parental responsibility and are thus irrelevant to mature children. There are, however, issues about parental behaviour, particularly contact, where older children might wish a court adjudication. Contact orders are limited in that they do not require the absent parent to spend time with the child, only the parent with care to permit this. A young person over 16 may be thought able to organise this without the court, although this ignores the emotional and other pressure which can be put on someone who has no other means of support. Requiring a parent to see a child may be thought likely to be counter-productive but failure to have this as an option weakens children's bargaining power and undermines the notion that contact is an important element of parenting.

The position of young people is not unlike that of wives before the wide availability and acceptance of divorce and the development of injunctive remedies. They must put up with their families as they are unless they can survive without them. Financial support may be obtained through the courts (or possibly the Child Support Agency) but other problems occur without the option of recourse to the courts and within context of conflicting messages about young people's dependence and independence.

Conclusion

Dependency is a major theme of the lives of children and young people but the dependence and consequent vulnerability of those over 16 is scarcely recognised in the Children Act 1989 because of the emphasis on the fading of

---

14 [1993] 1 FLR 832.
15 [1993] FLR 668.
16 [1993] 3 FLR 278.

parental responsibility as children's capacity develops. There are more limited powers to protect young people than children. In the past, those over 16, might have more easily protected themselves from family abuse by leaving home. Changes in the economic climate and, particularly, policies designed to extend the family's responsibility until at least the age of majority make such 'self rescue' extremely difficult. Access to all support services is more limited for young people in need than both those under 16 and adults who qualify for community care. Removal of state support is portrayed as strengthening the family but is motivated by a wish to reduce expenditure.

The responsibility of parents for their children is being extended throughout the period of secondary education to age 19 and generally whilst young people obtain training. There are suggestions too that this approach should apply to single parents under the age of 20[17] Parental responsibility in the legal sense is limited; it is largely restricted to reimbursing the state where benefit is claimed. Parent's status does not give parents power to control their children after the age of 16 except in rare circumstances. However, state control of young people continues through the power of the *parens patriae* jurisdiction to veto independent decisions which are viewed by the court as contrary to welfare.

For young people between the age 16 and 18 their relationships with their families are almost completely closed to the courts. Their independence derived from *Gillick* reinforces their dependence because the law has not provided a means for them to challenge their parents' actions. However, prolonged dependence of the young appears to be being recognised by the courts through their reluctance to accept that children have capacity to make decisions and the claim of greater power under *parens patriae*. Nevertheless, there remains a wide gulf between the legal view that children mature and become independent before their majority and the practical reality of dependence constructed by a shift of state resources away from this age group.

---

17   Michael Howard, Conservative Party Conference, October 1993.

Bibliography and References

Bainham, A	'The Privatisation of the Public Interest in Children' (1990) MLR 206
DH	'Caring for People: Community Care in the Next Decade and Beyond - Policy Guidance' (1990) Cm 839
DH	*Care Management and Assessment - Practitioners Guide* (1991)
DHSS	*Review of Child Care Law* (1985)
Eekelaar, J	'Parental Responsibility: State of Nature on Nature of the State' (1991) JSWFL 37-50.
Eekelaar, J	'The Emergence of Children's Rights' (1986) 6 Ox JLS 161-182
Finch, J	*Family Obligations and Social Change* (1989)
Fox-Harding, L	*Perspectives in Child Care Policy* (1992)
Health & Social Services Committee	'Sixth Report of the Parliamentary Health Committee, Community Care; The Way Forward' (1992-3) HCP 482
Harris, N	*Social Security for Young People* (1989)
Hunt, J	*Local Authority Wardships before the Children Act: The Baby or the Bathwater* (1993)
Jones, G & Wallace, C	*Youth, Family and Citizenship* (1992)
Law Commission	*Review of Child Law: Guardianship and Custody* (1988) HC 594
Masson, J	'Implementing Change for Children: Action at The Centre and Local Reaction' (1992) 19 J Law and Soc 320-338
Masson, J	'The Official Solicitor as the Child's Guardian ad Litem under the Children Act 1989' (1992) 4 J Ch L 58-62
Masson, J & Morton, S	'The Use of Wardship by Local Authorities' (1989) MLR 762-789
Sunkin, M	'Judicial Review and Part III of the Children Act 1989' (1992) 4 J Ch L 109-114

Chapter 2

New Provisions for Child Maintenance:
The Implications for Children and their Families

Penny Booth
University of Teesside

Once upon a time, a politician and a government department came up with a really super idea to cut the extensive expenditure on single parent families and, being terribly concerned about the millions spent on lone women with very young children in particular, set about creating (or did it all happen by accident?) a scheme to make men pay for their uncontrollable urges, and mothers for letting them have their wicked way. The taxes paid by good, old-fashioned families (the ones with 'values') would not in future, be diverted to support, in grand style, these profligates and their offspring. As a result, in true fairytale style, the world would be a better place.

Of course, we all know that this is not how it happened, but we can all believe in fairies at the bottom of the garden, and the briefest understanding of the how the Child Support Act 1991 was devised, and what is apparently intended by the new system, makes the fairytale version, for many, the preferred version. Time and space is not on my side on this occasion, and I suspect that many have already made themselves familiar to a certain extent with the provisions of the new legislation. For those much more familiar with some of the details than I am, I apologise if a brief introduction is boringly familiar.

The government's proposals in the White Paper 'Children come First' Cm 1264 published in 1990 were intended to ensure the following:

1   parents would honour responsibilities towards their children which involved financial matters;

2   there would be a 'fair' system which had regular reviews and consistent results;

3   dependence upon income support would be reduced;

4   parental incentives to work rather than be dependent upon the state would be provided;

5   the public would receive an efficient and effective service.

The aim to make all parents (more) responsible for their children follows from what may be seen as a three-fold attack upon what some political influences have seen as the 'regrettable' changing family roles, values and sociological norms in the late twentieth century.

Firstly, the Children Act of 1989, which, to put it simply, promoted the idea of children's rights and parental responsibilities, curtailing the powers of local authority social services and providing an underpinning of the Victorian 'good' family à la 1980s style.

Secondly, the practical side to this was further promoted by the provisions of the more recently lambasted Criminal Justice Act 1991, which made parents more responsible for the criminal acts of their offspring, as required by ss 56-58 of that Act. Admittedly, this latter provision has not had quite the force in the argument as the first and last. Thirdly, the Child Support Act of 1991 with its main aim of making parents responsible for the maintenance of their children brings into sharp relief a rather 'monetary' idea of what it may mean to be 'responsible' for ones children.

The perception of this three-pronged 'attack' is noted elsewhere.[1]

Debate during the report stage of the bill resulted in interesting comments upon the aim - that it was purported to be designed to benefit children, but that in both origin and intention it was: '... framed primarily to reduce expenditure'.[2]

Few would argue with the premise that children come first, or that parents ought to be responsible for them; or, indeed, that 'responsible' means a measure of financial outlay, presumably supported by the state where the alternatives are non-starters because parents simply do not have the financial means and the result would be that the children would otherwise suffer. However, it is clear that the provisions within the Child Support Act 1991 have created huge controversy in their application. There can be no doubt that children come expensive!

It has been estimated that for the one-parent family (for whom the pressures are tremendous) £3.5 billion was paid in social security payments during 1988-9, comparing rather alarmingly to an estimate of that being some three times the figure (in 1990 prices) of that paid six or seven years previous. If financial considerations alone were important, here is the argument for a reduction in the burden for the taxpayer. Within the Act there are draconian measures (such as the accumulation of liability to pay and the consequent debt, to the reduced benefit direction and measures for the caring parent to be encouraged to comply) to ensure the compliance of absent parents and carers, with little, if any, room for manoeuvre on the part of either the Child Support Officer or Agency, or that of the Child Support Appeal Tribunal, who, under s 20, will hear appeals on certain aspects of the provisions.

The Act came into force on 5 April 1993 and brought with it the Child Support Agency which works within the Department of Social Security.

---

1   I would note in particular the newspaper reports at the time of the 'launch' of the provisions and other sources referred to in the course of the paper.

2   Lord McGregor; but no doubt thought by many.

Eventually, the Agency will take over from the courts aspects of assessment, collection and enforcement of maintenance that relates to children. There will be few exceptions -namely 'top-up' maintenance for disabled children, school fees extras and where families and children are not living in this country. Basically, as had been pointed out elsewhere,[3] the discretion of the courts will be replaced by an inflexible administrative system whose officers will have enormous powers conferred upon them by the Act.

The most immediate aspect of this inflexibility will be the application of a rigid formula by the Agency to assess the amount payable by a parent for the upkeep of a child. The formula itself is complicated - and is well documented in the texts referred to earlier (under reference point 1) and in a number of articles already published.[4] Perhaps there is no need for me to go into the detail here, since it is so thoroughly dealt with elsewhere, for, as has been noted,

> 'The Child Support Act 1991 has all the hallmarks of the Department of Social Security and Treasury, and few of our carefully constructed system of child and family law'.[5]

The natural parents of a child are responsible for maintaining that child; when the parents no longer live together, then the parent who is not looking after the child on a day-to-day basis must pay child support through the Agency. A maintenance assessment form will be completed and the Agency will send out an enquiry form to the parent who is not looking after the child.

The rather tactless approach to the problems of deciding amounts payable for the maintenance of children are perhaps indicated and highlighted by the references to 'caring' parents and 'absent' parents, as though there were always some choice in the matter.

It would be easy to ask whether there was any real and helpful definition in terms other than the rather crude meanings assigned by the Act - that is, to service a scheme which applies a non-discretionary formula across the board. Schedule 1 to the Act gives details of the formula, although the uninitiated may wish to begin with an explanation which simplifies the formula, especially if algebra or mathematics was never your favourite subject at school.

The Schedule is added to the provisions within the regulations to the Act which contain the further detail essential to those who have the unenviable task of applying the formula in individual cases. For the purposes of the observations in this paper, it is only necessary for a reminder that the formula involves calculating the amount which is required to provide for the daily needs of the child who is the subject of the maintenance. This maintenance

---

3   See, for example, comments made by Wendy Mantle in her short guide to the Act.
4   Bird, Roger 'The Child Support Act 1991 - An Outline' November 1991 Fam Law 478.
5   Simpson, Jane and Spitz, Louise 'Paying up for Children' (1993) 24 March Gazette 90/12.

requirement is composed of the aggregate of income support personal allowance for the child, the income support family premium, adult income support personal allowance for a person aged over 25 where the child is 16 or under and lone parent premium, less child benefit payable.

Under s 8 of the Act either parent may apply for a maintenance assessment and s 4 of the Act provides for the authorisation of the Child Support Agency to make the assessment of the requirement and the amount the absent parent must pay. The word 'authorise' is worth returning to later.

There are estimates (by the Child Support Agency) that the level of maintenance payable will rise considerably for many. Incomes and necessary outgoings of each parent are applied to the maintenance requirement and the formula is used to arrive at the figure that the absent parent must pay for child support. Within the formula there are provisions to ensure that the paying parent is not left with too little money; by the same token, the very rich paying parent will pay further sums in addition to the calculated amount in order that the child shall benefit from the increased resources of the parent, and share in the greater wealth available.

Averages are not always helpful, but it would seem that there are estimates at this time of some 20 pounds per week for court order payments per child (the average in my own area, when there is an absent parent in work to pay, are nearer 15 to 18 pounds per week) applying at present with probable increases to around 60 pounds under the formula. Large increases can be held to 20 pounds per week for the first year only, thereafter the powers of the Agency will be applied to ensure that the full increase payable will be forthcoming.Trevor Berry, of Families Need Fathers said: 'However many powers the Agency has, it can't get money that is not there.'[6]

Parents looking after children and receiving Income Support, Family Credit or Disability Working Allowance are obliged to co-operate with the Agency investigation into the means of the absent parent unless a s 6 exemption is applicable. Section 6(1) and 6(2) exempts claiming parents from co-operation (the use of the Agency collection and enforcement services) if there are reasonable grounds for believing that compliance would involve a risk of harm or undue distress to the caring parent of the child concerned. The extent of this distress is not yet known, and is sure to be the subject of appeal to the Child Support Appeal Tribunal in due course. If the formula itself is causing confusion and dismay in legal circles, then this exemption will cause far more for the parent who fears to encourage contact with the absent parent, or who has had little or no contact since the conception of the child, if, indeed, there is any wish to have further contact at all. There may be many who consider that it is not enough simply to blithely suggest that all this should have been considered before contemplating the act that led to the conception

---

6   Berry, Trevor *The Guardian* (1993) 19 January.

at all; most human beings, I would suggest, are not so calculating. Even if they were, it hardly justifies the potential suffering on the part of the children and families concerned.

A refusal to make an application (or to co-operate with an assessment where information is required on the absent parent, and after a period of consideration of up to six weeks) will result in a loss of benefit over 26 weeks of 20% of the personal Income Support allowance payable to a 25-year-old or over (whatever the parental age) and a loss of 10% over a further 52 weeks. Child Support Officers have been told that the parent with care must be believed unless their story is improbable or there is evidence to suggest that they could co-operate without 'undue harm or distress'.

The Reduced Benefit Direction will be a considerable loss for a parent surviving on welfare benefits. It applies until a tribunal hearing date has been set, with a reimbursement if the caring parent is successful at the hearing.

This lack of choice for those dependent upon welfare benefits, and the particularly punitive nature of the penalty, has given cause for concern among welfare rights workers, solicitors and those with an academic interest in the application of the provisions. At this time, it is anticipated that those not in receipt of state benefits have a choice as to whether or not to apply for a maintenance assessment through the provisions under the Act. By 1996 all parents in whatever categories included within the provisions will have been brought into the 'rolling programme' which has begun with 'new' benefit cases requiring financial support from absent parents. Whilst this is undoubtedly a slow start, success in the application of this formula funding may encourage the inclusion of the same to those situations previously and still, right now, intended to be dealt with by the courts. There would seem to be only scant argument to exclude other cases from the Act where it 'works,'especially when it is considered that the same arguments did not prevent the application of the formula in the first place.

In relation to decisions taken, under s 2 of the Act the Child Support Officer must 'have regard to the welfare of any child likely to be affected by his decision.' This only applies where there is any element of discretion and it does not say that the officer must regard the welfare of the child as being a first or most important consideration. The Reduced Benefit Direction under s 46 is likely to lead to a great deal of anxiety - that alone cannot be to the benefit of any child. Guidelines given to officers advocate 'care and sensitivity' but interviews will still have to take place so that sufficient information may be forthcoming to allow informed decisions to take place. It is anticipated that examples of 'approved' non-co-operation might include a fear of violence (especially where there is evidence such as previous attacks), the child concerned being conceived as a result of incest or rape, or the fear of sexual abuse. The address of the parent with care does not have to be revealed to the absent parent, however. Cases will, it is understood, be dealt with individually, although a desire on the part of the parent with care to ensure that the absent parent never has contact with the child is unlikely to be regarded as sufficient reason for non-co-operation with the Agency. Contact is a separate issue from the payment of maintenance, but solicitors may feel that the two issues have often been regarded as connected.

Other issues in relation to the punitive nature of the Act include the effects upon the families themselves of these assessments. The larger sums likely to be payable have been noted[7] and the pressures upon both parents even where the parent in receipt of the sums has had no choice in the decision to collect the extra, will not assist the healthy development of family relationships or the return to health of strained relationships in the aftermath of separation. There may be those who would say that it is not the role of these provisions to improve such situations, but it cannot be denied that if the Act is meant to be for the benefit of the child, then that particular aim is under attack from the very provisions designed to achieve it. The impetus for wishing to make parents pay derives from the growing numbers dependent upon welfare benefits - especially the numbers of one parent families headed by women whose male partners, by choice or not, do not share the family home with the woman and the children. It cannot be as cheap to finance two households as one (even if the male lives in a bedsit) and young children are frequently looked after by women who are unable to seek work outside the home. Many such family situations involve the payment of welfare benefits, but it could be argued that a more extensive application of the interim measure of s 8 of the Social Security Act 1990 may have achieved more in that direction without the necessity to use the proverbial sledgehammer to crack a nut!

When the Act is fully established the courts will lose most of their current responsibilities for child maintenance. The experience of years of decisions based upon a whole picture gleaned from the often sorry circumstances presented in court will be lost to family and child law, because it will not be possible to utilise it. The courts will retain responsibility for deciding with whom a child will live and issues related to the child such as contact with the child, support of a former spouse, property issues and disputed paternity, in addition to other less 'immediate' matters.

The Act is an uneasy bedfellow with the Children Act 1989, for under those provisions orders will only be made where there is argument for making an order at all, rather than relying upon agreement between the parties. Where is the agreement with the Child Support Act? The powers of the Agency (s 15 inspectors, and powers and sanctions in ss 31, 33, 35, 40 and 43) are extensive, and include those to search property, inspect documents and obtain

---

7   Bird, Roger 'Child Support Act 1991 - An Outline' (1991) Fam Law 478; Rae, Maggie 'Caring Parents and Absent Parents' (1993) NLJ 513; Burrows, David 'Child Support Act 1991 - Why we Need to Know About It' (1992) Fam Law 342; Eekelaar, John 'Child Support - An Evaluation' (1991) Fam Law 511.

information from tax offices, housing benefit departments, social security and so on. Allegedly undisclosed information can be investigated prior to any tribunal hearing and failure to give relevant information may be effectively 'punished' by an interim assessment of twice the standard assessment to be applied until the full information is provided. Courts are unable to exercise power which they would otherwise have had to 'make, vary or revive' a maintenance order in relation to a child or absent parent. The existence of a maintenance agreement does not prevent either parent from applying under the provisions of the Act for an assessment.

It has been noted elsewhere[8] that the provision to seek an assessment even after suitable arrangements have already been made in relation to maintenance will cause dismay among practitioners, it is likely to cause far more dismay among those clients who have settled (or had hoped to settle) arrangements involving the 'clean break' under ss 25 and 25A of the Matrimonial Causes Act 1973. Whilst this was considered by the Law Commission Working Party[9] and the availability of welfare benefits was 'tuned into the system,' as it were, the clean break was obviously popular. The compensation for (usually) the husband was reduced periodical payments, or termination of payments to the wife, though the clean break applied only to the partner, not to the children. Now there will be little, if any, inducement to settle if at any time in the future it would be open to either partner to ask the Agency to make an assessment (which includes a sum for the partner themselves) which the court could not then overturn.

There may be ways around this difficulty[10] but clearly many practitioners will be wary of encouraging the court to consider a clean break, at least in the early period of the imposition of the Act, in the knowledge of a strong suspicion that someone has changed the goal-posts:

> 'The Child Support Act ... appears to mark a significant turning-point in the direction of legal regulation of the family ... The prevailing wisdom was that there should be less scrutiny by the court of the circumstances in which a marriage breakdown occurred, greater attention paid to the encouragement of agreements reached by parents through negotiation in private, and trust in parents to put their children's interests first.'[11]

The overall punitive atmosphere to this Act may well rebound considerably upon the children of the relationship, rather than be seen, as the government hoped, as a fairer and consistent approach to the payment of maintenance for children.

8　Hayes, Mary 'Making and Enforcing Child Maintenance Obligations' (1991) Fam Law 105.

9　'The Financial Consequences of Divorce' (1981) 112.

10　Clout, Imogen 'Child Support Act 1991 - the Implications for Divorce Solicitors' (1993) Fam Law 236.

11　Douglas, Gillian 'Child Support: the Legislation'.

What of government policy towards the family in the 1990s? Who can argue against the view that 'responsible parenthood' brings a heavy burden?

'Encouraging responsible fatherhood rather than discouraging single mothers must be at the heart of government policy to revitalise the family.'[12]

In the same article it was reported that Patricia Hewitt of the Institute for Public Policy Research said that the government was concentrating upon fathers as the absent parent (admittedly, statistically this is likely to be the case) and dwelling upon their financial responsibilities. This was matched by a failure to place emphasis on needs to 'integrate fathers in the lives of their children'.

'Integration' implies much more than putting hands into pockets especially where it may be reluctantly, or somebody else's hand, and is hardly a natural progression from the provisions and aims of the Children Act. Parental responsibility is more than an emphasis upon financial responsibility. Might it not be that some fathers will feel that the financial emphasis both gives them the right to demand their money's worth, yet absolves them from other manifestations of their parental responsibility, in a more insidious manner than maintenance was previously viewed as 'buying into' the supposed right to access? There are, already, many opportunities for acrimony in the breakdown of a relationship. They may have been increased rather than reduced.

It has been suggested that the introduction of this mechanism for the arrival at a figure for maintenance for the children of the relationship could be so successful in terms of the savings made upon welfare benefits and legal aid for court time that its extension into other areas of family dispute is only a matter of time. Government alarm at the large financial outlay (hence the desire to cut back on Legal Aid) for parties, in these disputes (many of whom are female) might be more attractive than supporting the continuing parenthood and participatory decision-making that is apparently ousted by non-discretionary formula approaches to these problems.

Legal Aid is already under attack, and new proposals for divorce make the likelihood of cut-backs 'to the bone' where family matters are concerned a probability awaiting a certainty. There is concern about the burden of time and money placed upon the court system. Why not a formula funded system for fixing all maintenance and property matters? We may consider that the complexities would be too much, and that the government would not risk the reaction. Many would have thought as much about child support.

It may be so that:

---

12   Burt, Alistair the social security minister in an interview with *The Times* (1993) 1 June.

'... the Agency is not about returning the traditional British family to its rightful pedestal or about curbing unwanted pregnancies'.[13]

However, it is about saving money, and its success would encourage similar approaches to be taken to other aspects of family and child law. Any inconsistencies with previous legislation or aims will not overshadow a desire to curb expenditure.

In the increasingly complex society in which we now find ourselves, and within which family and child law operates, there appears to be imposed an inflexible system without much discretion, which has financial calculation at its heart and little consideration as to whether there is any promotion of real stability in families during and after separation. One wonders whether there has been any development and progress in the last few decades, and whether the Children Act 1989 ever happened at all. Perhaps a more vital consideration is the extent to which we would consider, after a brief look at the application of the Child Support Act provisions and some of the implications for children and their families, whether this Act has done much at all to support the claim that 'children come first'.

---

13 Hepplewhite, Ross Head of the Child Support Agency.

Bibliography and References

There are a number of texts now published on the Child Support Act 1991.

It is difficult to recommend one in particular, since much depends upon your requirements. The following are very useful, and contain explanation or commentary, although detail varies.

Some articles are referred to in this paper which may provide the required detail in themselves.

Jacobs, Edward & Douglas, Gillian	*Child Support: The Legislation Commentary* (1993) Sweet and Maxwell
Bird, Roger	*Child Maintenance - The Child Support Act*
Burrows, David	*The Child Support Act - A Practitioner's Guide* (1993) Butterworths
Mantle, Wendy	*Child Support: The New System Explained* (1993) Longman Practitioner Series
Bird, Roger	'The Child Support Act 1991 - An Outline' November (1991) Fam Law 478
Simpson, Jane & Spitz, Louise	'Paying up for Children' (1993) Gazette 90/12
Berry, Trevor	*The Guardian* 19 January 1993.
Rae, Maggie	'Caring Parents and Absent Parents' New Law Journal (1993) 513
Burrows, David	'Child Support Act 1991 - Why We Need to Know About It' (1992) Fam Law 342
Eekelaar, John	'Child Support - An Evaluation' (1991) December Fam Law 511
Hayes, Mary	'Making and Enforcing Child Maintenance Obligations' (1991) Fam Law 105
Clout, Imogen	'Child Support Act 1991 - the Implications for Divorce Solicitors' (1993) Fam Law 236
Jacobs, Edward & Douglas, Gillian	*Child Support: The Legislation*
Burt, Alistair	The social security minister in an interview with *The Times* 1 June 1993
Law Commission	'The Financial Consequences of Divorce' (1981) Paper No 112

Chapter 3

ChildTax

Roger Cockfield, Reader in Taxation
Mary Mulholland, Senior Lecturer in Law
De Montfort University, Leicester

This paper is based on an article by the authors published in Butterworths' *Tax Journal* and reproduced by kind permission of the Editor.

In July 1990, the then Prime Minister announced the intention to ' set up a new Child Support Agency which will have access to the information necessary to trace absent parents and make them accept their financial obligations ... assessing maintenance through a standard administrative formula ...'. In the summary to the White Paper 'Children Come First' it is pointed out that there are inconsistent decisions about how much maintenance should be paid, that only 30% of lone mothers receive regular maintenance for their children and that 750,000 lone parents depend on income support. The purpose of this article is to look at the tax aspects of the resulting Child Support Act 1991.

An individual's liability to UK income tax has depended as much on his personal circumstances as the amount he earned or the profits he made. The income liable to tax is reduced by a number of allowances before being charged to tax. The amount of personal allowances is dependent on a person's marital status, age and previously, the number of children. This latter allowance was abolished in the late 1970s to be replaced by the present non-taxable child benefit. The benefit of the 1970s child allowance was given to the father by a reduction in his tax bill, whereas today's child benefit is paid to the mother. Further allowances in respect of mortgage interest paid and pension contributions are available to reduce the tax bill. From 6 April 1993, there are two important changes brought about by the Child Support Act 1991. Firstly, certain individuals will now pay extra tax if they are separated or divorced and their children are living with their former partner. Secondly the Department of Social Security (DSS) (through the Child Support Agency (CSA)) becomes a Revenue Raising Department in its own right, collection of NIC having been made through the Inland Revenue. Only those unfortunate enough to be unemployed or on low income will have had the experience of dealing with the DSS; this will now be extended to those on substantial incomes for the very first time. They will have to learn to deal with a department whose philosophy is based on dealing with benefit cases. The CSA has powers of making assessments, collecting tax and an appeals mechanism that duplicates the General Commissioners (but does not mirror them exactly). This involves a huge duplication of resources, which it is doubted, will even remotely reach the level of cost-effectiveness of either the Inland Revenue or Customs and Excise.

Is Child Support Maintenance (CSM) a tax? A narrow definition of a tax is any form of compulsory levy by central or local government. One of the characteristics by which a body can be identified as a government is its ability to levy taxes. A broader definition is a compulsory levy (either distinct or in the form of higher prices) by any body which is given monopoly powers by central government. Thus excessive prices (by comparison with other countries) for electricity, phones and food (through the CAP) are examples of private taxation. CSM is a true tax in that the recipient will frequently be no better off, suffering a pound for pound reduction in benefits. Once this stage is passed, CSM becomes more like a private tax. All taxes involve the transfer of income or capital from one group of persons to another group (which may involve some of the paying group). CSM is also misnamed as the recipient is the mother and there is no guarantee that the extra money, if any, will be spent on the children. Another novel area is that unlike Inland Revenue (IR) and Customs and Excise (C&E), the CSA charges the taxpayer £44 for the privilege of an assessment and £34 for collection of the tax. The receiving parent will also have to pay these sums. These charges are waived for those on low income, and the collection charge can be avoided by not using the CSA collection service.

The concept of 'making absent fathers pay for their children's maintenance' and 'children come first' are noble ones. It is debatable and indeed doubtful whether the CSA will achieve its original aims. The CSA would appear to be a cynical manipulation of these concepts. For the majority on Income Support or Family Credit, the loss of those benefits when they receive CSM means they are personally no better off.

The CSA will so alienate many fathers, that not only will any vestige of responsibility be destroyed, but in extreme cases the children of fathers who had a working relationship with their former partners and who were paying maintenance agreed between the parties, will now suffer, due to the resentment caused by the imposition of CSM. In extreme cases violence will be used against their former spouses. If £400 of Poll Tax could cause riots and high levels of civil disobedience, just consider what £4,000 of Child Tax will do.

Retrospective legislation is unattractive at the best of times. For those who made generous capital settlements in exchange for no or low maintenance, the CSA will be their financial ruin. It represents the undoing of final settlements based on the clean break principle. The tax is unfair in that the amount you pay depends, not on the needs of your children, nor your own income but whether your ex-spouse is prepared to work or not. Many marriages have foundered due to the non-commitment of the former spouse to the marriage. That non-commitment should not be rewarded after divorce. The real absconding fathers will not be brought to heel, those who never intended to pay will still avoid payment by going unknown, moving around a lot or even changing their names. The demand for second identities will increase.

A new form of legal avoidance

From the Government which introduced 'can't pay, won't pay' as the poor man's legal avoidance for poll tax, we now meet violence as a new form of legal avoidance. Mothers will not have to name the biological father if they are at risk. Whether threats of violence or actual violence are needed are not clear. It is also unclear whether one black eye is sufficient or whether it requires one black eye plus two teeth knocked out. Men should know whether one or multiple beatings are required. The CSA should publish a tariff of what they regard as an acceptable level of violence to satisfy the requirements of s 6(2) of the Child Support Act. Again it is not clear whether the violence must be carried out by the biological father or whether a stand-in is acceptable.

Examples

The amount of CSM is made up of a Basic Element, which is paid at 50% of Assessable Income until the Basic Element is met, plus an Additional Element which is paid at 25% of Assessable Income subject to an upper limit. All figures are worked on a weekly basis.

The Basic Element is calculated as follows for two children age 11 and 14.

Child Allowance for each (*under 11 – £15.05; 11-15; – £22.15; 16-17 – £26.45*; 18 – £34.80**) * if still at school	2 x £22.15	£44.30
Family Premium		£9.65
Lone Parent (if Care Parent has no partner)		£4.90
Adult Allowance (if any child under 16)		£44.00
Less Child Benefit (£10 + £8.10)		**£102.85** £18.10
		£84.75

This will be met in full when the Absent Parent has Assessable Income of £169.50 (50% of 169.50 =84.75), thereafter he pays Additional Element at 25% of Assessable Income.

Assessable Income of Absent parent	Basic Element (50%)	Additional Element at 25%	Total
£100 per week	£50.00	nil	£50.00
£150 per week	£75.00	nil	£75.00
£200 per week	£84.75	£7.62 (25% {200-2 x 84.75})	£92.38
£300 per week	£84.75	£32.63 (25% {300-2 x 84.75})	£113.38

The upper limit of the additional element is computed as follows. For each child, add to the age geared child allowance the family premium; then multiply the result by three. The overall upper limit will be this figure plus the basic element. For one child of 18 still at school, this works out at £8,980 pa. For three children aged 11,16 and 18, the total upper limit is about £23,000. It is difficult to see why there is an upper limit at all. If the father earns a million pounds per year, why should his children not receive the same automatic bounty as the rest.

Assessable Income is income from all sources *after* tax, NIC and 50% of pension contributions *less* Exempt Income. Exempt Income is the Adult Allowance of £44 plus allowances for children who live with that parent *plus* housing costs ie rent or mortgage payments. In the examples given here, it is assumed that the children do not live at all with the Absent Parent and that the Care Parent does not work. If the Care Parent works and/or the children are shared, the payments are reduced. For these situations refer to the Booklets issued by the CSA 'For Parents Who Live Apart' CSA 2001 and 'Notes For Advisers' CSA 2018.

The following table shows the average and marginal rates of tax after the introduction of ChildTax. Payroll (ie earnings plus employers NIC) is used so that comparison can easily be made whether the person is employed or self-employed. The employee on a payroll of £24,111 suffers a total NIC tax of £4,023, whereas his self-employed counterpart with profits of the same figure pays only £1,265. NIC is a tax on payroll while ultimate burden is borne by the employee.

ChildTax
Average and Marginal Tax Rates

Payroll	NIC	Income tax	Child Tax	Average Rate	Marginal Rate
50	nil	nil	nil	nil	nil
60	4	nil	1	8	48
70	5	nil	4	14	48
80	7	2	7	19	57
90	8	4	9	24	57
100	11	6	11	28	65
120	14	10	16	33	59
140	17	14	21	37	61
180	25	23	29	43	61
200	29	28	33	4	63

This table is based on the following: two children 11 and 14, absent parent is single, care parent does not work, mortgage is 6% (net) of three times annual earnings. ChildTax is 50% of first £170 of assessable income, then 25% of excess. Accessible income is payroll less NIC, IT, mortgage. Payroll is earnings plus employers NIC. Taxes are NIC+IT+ChildTax. An extract from the spreadsheet program used to calculate these figures is shown at Appendix A. The example Bertie, at Appendix B, shows a complete calculation of income tax, NIC and Child Tax. It also demonstrates how no account is taken of the capital settlement of the fact there is no obligation on the ex-wife to work.

CSM will be phased in over three years starting with those cases where there is no existing maintenance agreement, then those where the care parent is on Income Support or Family Credit. Finally from the 8 April 1996, those cases where there is an existing maintenance agreement and the Care Parent is not on benefit. This last group will be taken on in three month blocks according to the first letter of the surname. The phasing in of the CSA is unfair. Consider the outcry there would be if an increase in pensions was paid to surnames A-C this month, but W-Z did not get their increase until next year with no back-dating. The courts have so far blocked attempts by ex-wives to set-aside their existing court orders, so that the CSA can take up their case immediately.

The CSA may also be a backdoor method of withdrawing tax relief of maintenance payments under the old (pre-15/3/88) rules. Under the old rules, it was common practice to pay maintenance direct to the children so that their personal allowances would cover the recipient family's tax liability eg, Archie paid £3,445 to each of his three children who lived with their mother following divorce under a court order made in 1987. Archie still gets tax relief at both basic and higher rates on the £10,335 paid.

Under the CSA, if Archie is ordered to pay £3,446 for each child, it will be paid direct to the mother. The Revenue claim (in leaflet IR 93 at p 11) that tax relief will be limited to £1,720 (or nil if the mother has remarried). This view is based on s 36 FA 1988 which states that the 'new' rules apply where there is a change in the persons to whom the maintenance is paid. Assuming Archie is a higher rate taxpayer and that his ex-wife has remarried, the loss of tax relief will cost Archie £4,134 (10,335 @ 40%). In this extreme example his ex is only £3 better off at cost to Archie of over £4,000.

Can Archie claim to fulfil his obligations under s 1 of the CSA 1991 by paying £10.335 to the children and £3 to the mother making the total of £10,338 required by the CSA. There is some support for this view in s 9(2) which states 'nothing in this Act shall be taken to prevent entering into a maintenance agreement which in subsection (1) includes payment to the child. In this way Archie will retain tax relief on the £10,335.

Income Tax is a progressive tax, starting off at nil% (the area of the personal allowances and allowable deductions like pension contributions), then 20% (the reduced rate band), 25% (basic rate band) with the rest of the income taxed at the higher rate of 40%. VAT is often presented as a progressive tax with a nil rate band (on food and housing) followed by a standard rate of 17.5% (on other goods and services). The argument is that the poor spend most on the basics of life (which are zero rated) but in reality VAT is a heavier burden as a percentage of their total expenditure. The proposed introduction of VAT on domestic heating illustrates this. VAT is a mildly regressive tax.

The tax is highly regressive in two ways. First, the progressive rates are reversed compared to income tax. One starts off paying at 50% of assessable income, then 25% and finally nil percent. Secondly, the overall percentage pay declines as one goes up the income scale.

The Conservative Party has made great electoral noise about the negative motivation of high rates of tax. It is surprising to find they have extended the direct tax system to introduce marginal tax rates of over 60%.

The general rule for expenses for the self-employed is found in SI 1815, Schedule 1 Part 1 para 3(3)(a) which states '... any expenses which are *reasonably incurred* and are wholly and exclusively defrayed for the purpose of the business'.

Traders are allowed to deduct a very wide variety of business expenses for income tax purposes provided they are not directly for personal benefit, not entertaining and not capital expenditure. Capital expenditure covers the purchase of new premises, machinery and cars. Instead of depreciation on the last two, the Revenue allow their equivalent called capital allowances though the rates will be different. The expenses rule for traders is in practice very generous, whilst for employees it is notoriously strict. Under CSA, the business expenses must also be reasonable to be deducted. There is no guidance on what is meant by reasonable. There is considerable variation in the interpretation of reasonable by the Inland Revenue compared to the VAT boys (to establish a reasonable excuse to escape a VAT penalty is nigh impossible). Hazarding a guess much sponsorship expenditure will fall foul of this new rule (unable to link expenditure to increased sales) as will the running expenses of exotic cars (really a matter of personal choice and ego boosting). Conferences in exotic places and sales trips to the South of France will also be disallowed unless a viable business link can be demonstrated.

This is a much stricter rule than for Income Tax, much closer to the 'necessary' condition of Schedule E. There are further surprises in the expenses which are not allowed by para 3(4)(b);

'(iii)   the depreciation of any capital asset

(v)   any loss incurred before the start of the period of accounts

(vii)   any loss incurred in any other trade, profession or vocation'.

There does not appear to be any scheme of capital allowances on any form of plant and machinery etc. There does not appear to be any scheme for the relief of losses brought forward or from another trade on a current year basis. I do not need to spell out how disastrous these provisions will be for the self-employed, nor the unfortunate precedent they set if the Inland Revenue decides to copy them to the Income Tax code.

Let us look at the anti-avoidance powers which para 9 of Schedule 1 of the Act authorises the Secretary of State to make regulations about. These are so wide and vague, there may be doubts as to their constitutional authority. The introduction of general anti-avoidance provisions will be a novel one for most accountants and tax advisers who rarely deal with welfare cases. It is disturbing that the rules can be changed by Statutory Instrument, which usually have a non-existent level of scrutiny in Parliament.

Paragraph 26 of Schedule 1 Part 5 provides that where a person has performed a service for less than full remuneration to reduce his assessable income, the COS estimate of the amount of remuneration foregone shall be deemed to be his income. Whilst there are let-outs for work done for charities and voluntary organisations, beware the solicitor who offers free advice on the golf course to his fellow golfers. This paragraph extends the principle of *Sharkey v Wherner* to the provision of services for both the employed and self-employed.

Paragraph 27 states:

'... where the child support officer is satisfied that ... a person has intentionally deprived himself of

(a) any income or capital which would otherwise be a source of income

(b) any income or capital which it would be reasonable to expect would be secured by him

with a view to reducing the amount of his assessable income, his income shall include the amount foregone or deprived as estimated by the child support officer.'

There is no guidance on how the estimates will be made or in what circumstances this paragraph will apply. Paragraph 30 allows the attributed capital to be reduced by the national income each year. There are tremendous implications for all tax planning schemes especially deeds of variation. How far will the Courts interpret this for poor business deals or even deals not consummated?

If another person (including partner) does the depriving, this paragraph cannot bite. What is meant by 'intentionally' is open to doubt. The paragraph refers to a source of income. Schemes to reduce the amount of income whilst retaining the source would appear not to be caught. What is meant by source? Does it take the same meaning as for income tax ie a property is the source, whilst the rents are the income (or profits) that flow from that source.

Does this cover the switching of investments? Suppose I have £20,000 to invest. Am I allowed to invest in a low coupon, high discount stock or must I invest (or deemed to have) in a high yield stock not issued at a discount? There is silence on whether non taxable income from National Savings Certificates etc are income for CSA purposes. How will the CSO estimate the amount of income? On what basis, is the decision appealable? Tariff income (p 13 of NI 196) suggests £1 per week for each £250 of capital. This works out at 20% - a fantastic rate of return.

Section 20 TMA 1970 contains extensive powers for the Inland Revenue to call for documents of taxpayers. These powers are subject to the supervision of the Special/General Commissioners. Professional privilege of barristers and solicitors is specifically recognised in s 20B(8). The power of entry onto premises is more tightly controlled requiring the permission of a Circuit Judge and again professional privilege is recognised.

There is no equivalent control by the courts or recognition of professional privilege in the CSA against an Inspector acting under s 15. That Inspector could enter the offices of a solicitor or accountant acting for an absent parent and require answers to any questions and the supply of any document. Failure to co-operate can result in a fine on summary conviction not exceeding level 3 on the standard scale. Although there was criticism of these draconian powers in the House of Lords (Official Report 19 March 1992 column 558), the Lord Chancellor thought them necessary. It is amazing that Parliament will provide proper control of Civil Servants and Police in some areas but not in others. Even Customs and Excise recognise professional privilege! Under s 15 there is no right of silence (except to take the 5th amendment) and no definition of reasonable excuse.

What defence mechanisms are available? Depending on how hard you want to play it, the first line is to deny being the biological father of the child. Note this is different from being regarded as the father of the child who is treated as a child of the family for matrimonial purposes. It has been estimated that a significant percentage of children are born to parents where the father is not the biological father. This is the reason why hospitals only take the blood group of the mother. The potential psychological damage to the children should not be underestimated, but this is one of the reasons why, with so much money at stake, this act is evil.

Appendix A

This appendix is an extract of the spreadsheet program used to generate the table showing average and marginal rates of tax at different levels of income. It makes considerable use of 'IF Statements' to automatically take into account the different rates of NIC at different levels of earnings (earnings are in cell C4). Let me explain the formula in cell D4. This says that if earnings (ie C4) are less than £54 per week, then NIC is nil; it then says if earnings are greater than £54 per week but less than £405, then the NIC is 9% of the earnings over £54 plus 2% of the first £54; if earnings are greater than £405 (the upper earnings limit) the NIC is £32.67. Cell E4 calculates personal income tax. If earnings (ie cell C4) are less than £66.25 (the weekly amount of the personal allowance), tax is nil; then if earnings are less than £104.71 (the weekly amount of the personal allowance plus reduced rate band), the tax is 20% of the earnings in the reduced rate band; the next part of the IF Statement deals with the basic rate taxpayer. Cell B4 calculates the employers NIC which is based on earnings. This is added to the earnings figure to give the total cost to the employer of that employee, this is called the payroll cost. Both employers and employees NIC are a form of payroll tax, complicated and with unfair marginal rates.

:A1:	'Weekly
:B1:	'Employers
:C1:	'Earnings
:D1:	'Employees
:E1:	'Tax
:F1:	'Child
:G1:	'Total
:H1:	'% of
:I1:	'Mortgage
:J1:	'Assessable
:K1:	'What's
:A2:	'Payroll
:B2:	'NIC
:D2:	'NIC
:F2:	'Care
:G2:	'Taxes
:H2:	'Payroll
:I2:	'or Rent
:J2:	'Income
:K2:	'Left
:B3:	'10.4% Rate

:E3:   'Basic Rate
:A4:   225
:B4:   +A4*10.4(100+10.4)
:C4:   +A4-B4
:D4:   @IF(C4<54,0,@IF(C4<405,0.09*(C4-54)+0.02*54,32.67))
:E4:   @IF(C4<66.25,0,@IF(C4<104.71,0.2*(C4-66.25),),.25*(C4-
         (3445+2000)/52)+0.2*2000/52))
:F4:   @IF(J4<169.5,0.5*J4,0.25*(J4-169.5)+84.75)
:G4:   +B4+D4+E4+F4
:H4:   100*G4/A4
:I4:   0.08*(52*C4*2/52)
:J4:   @IF(+D4-D4-E4-I4-44<0,0,D4-D4-E4-I4-44)
:K4:   +A4-G4-I4
:A5:   250
:B5:   +A5*10.4/(100+10.4)
:C5:   +A5-B5
:D5:   @IF(C5<54,0,@IF(C5<405,0.09*(C5-54)+0.02*54,32.67))
:E5:   @IF(C5<66.25,0,@IF(C5<104.71,0.2*(C5-66.25),0.25*(C5-
         (3445+2000)/52)+0.2*2000/52))
:F5:   @IF(J5<169.5,0.5*J5,0.25*(J5-169.5)+84.75)
:G5:   +B5+D5+E5+F5
:H5:   100*G5/A5
:I5:   0.08*(52*C5*2/52)
:J5:   @IF(+C5-D5-E5-I5-44<0,0,C5-D5-E5-I5-44)
:K5:   +A5-G5-I5

Appendix B

Bertie is an accountant who decides to become a bursar at £12,740 pa at a
public school following his redundancy from one of the large firms of
accountants. He is especially pleased to find that he is offered rent free
accommodation. He gave his house to his ex wife as part of a clean-break
settlement in exchange for no maintenance for her or their 11 year old child.
His ex wife decides to give up work as she has moved in with the senior
partner of his old firm who earns £300.000 pa.

The CSA will assess Archie as follows:

Child Allowance 1 under 15	£22.15
Family payment	9.65
Lone Parent	4.90
Adult Allowance (child under 16)	44.00

	80.70
Less Child Benefit	10.00

BMR	**£70.70**
Payroll	£14,065
Less Employers NIC (10.4% of £12,740)	1,325
Earnings	12,740
Less Employees NIC	950
Less Income Tax	2,199

	9,591
Less Exempt Income (£44pw x 52)	2,288

ASSESSABLE INCOME PER ANNUM	**£7,303**

or **£140.42 per week**

CHILD TAX at 50% is £3,651 pa pr £70.21 per week.

$$\frac{\text{Total Taxes}}{\text{Payroll}} = \frac{1325+950+2199=3651}{14,065} = \frac{8,125}{14,065} = \mathbf{57.8\%}$$

Archie's average rate of tax is 57.8% and his marginal rate is 67%. (9% NIC+25% Basic Rate+33% Child Tax (50% of 100 -9 -25).

Earnings	£12,740
less Personal Allowance	3,445

TAXABLE INCOME	**£9,295**
Reduced Rate(£2,500 @ 20%)	£ 500
Basic Rate (£6,795 @ 25%)	1,699

INCOME TAX	**£2,199**

Appendix C

Jack the Lad got around a bit when he was a young man. As a result he has three children aged 12, 13 and 14 all by different mothers, none of whom want the bother of working. Jack lives in a rent free caravan on the construction site he manages. His salary is £34,978.

The BASIC MAINTENANCE REQUIREMENT is

Child Allowance I under 15	£22.15
Family Payment	9.65
Lone Parent	4.90
Adult Allowance (child under 16)	44.00

	80.70
Less Child Benefit	10.00

BMR	£70.70
Multiply by three children	x 3
	£212.10
Payroll	£38,616
Less Employers NIC (10.4% of £34,978)	3,638

Earnings	34,978
Less Employees NIC (Max)	1,699
Less Income Tax	8.933

Net Income	24,346
Less Exempt Income (£44pw x 52)	2,288

ASSESSABLE INCOME PER ANNUM	**£22,058**

or **£424.19 per week**

CHILD TAX at 50% is £11,029 pa or £212.09 per week

$$\frac{\text{Total Taxes}}{\text{Payroll}} = \frac{3638+1699+8933+11029}{38,616} = \frac{25,299}{38,616} = \textbf{65.6\%}$$

If all children by same mother, then BMR is £98.80
(£70.70 plus 2CA @ £22.15 - 2CB @ £8.10)

CHILD TAX at 50% of £197.80 is	£98.90
plus at 25% of (£424.19 - £197.80) is	56.60

	£155.50

Jack would save **£57** per week if all his children had the same mother

Earnings	£34,978
less Personal Allowance	3,445

TAXABLE INCOME	**£31,533**
Reduced Rate 2,500 @ 20%	£ 500
Basic Rate 21,200 @ 25%	5,300
Higher Rate 7,833 @ 40%	3,133

INCOME TAX	**£8,933**

Chapter 4

Law and the Altruistic Child in Medicine

Linda Delany LLB MJur
The Manchester Metropolitan University

The pages of *Hello!* do not perhaps commonly inspire conference papers on the law relating to children but their fully illustrated interview with the Ayala family in 1992 did provoke the reflections which follow here.

The facts of what I will call the Ayala case were as follows. Abe and Mary Ayala, a married couple living in California, considered their family complete after the birth of their daughter Anissa and their son Airon. Abe underwent a vasectomy. Then, at the age of 16, Anissa was diagnosed as suffering from leukaemia. Only a bone-marrow transplant could save her life, and sibling bone-marrow was likely to be the most suitable. When Airon's bone-marrow proved to be incompatible, Abe and Mary Ayala decided to have a third child in the hope that his or her bone-marrow would match Anissa's. Following the reversal of Abe's vasectomy, Mary became pregnant and in due course gave birth to daughter Marissa Eve. When the baby was old enough her bone-marrow was harvested and, backed up by foetal stem cells taken from the umbilical cord at birth, was transferred to Anissa. The medical intervention was, as far as I know, successful.

While *Hello!* enthused, predictably, over the good fortune of the Ayala family, other journalistic reports expressed unease at the concept of a made-to-order child produced for the sole purpose of helping a sibling. However, the validity in law of what was done to baby Marissa Eve received little attention and, as far as I know, no legal challenge was made on her behalf.

Bone-marrow donations by children, including very young children, to help siblings suffering from leukaemia are carried out in this country too. Parents and hospitals co-operate in this without recourse to the courts. This paper examines the legal aspects of this practice. Can parents give consent on their young child's behalf to a bone-marrow donation? Do cases need to be referred to court? Does the law limit the circumstances in which young children may display their altruism? The answers to these questions turn out to be uncomfortably unclear. This paper therefore goes on to recommend that there should be clear guidance on these issues and that there should be safeguards in the system to protect children from being 'volunteered' where this is inappropriate.

Bone-marrow donations by young children have attracted no specific legislation. They are not covered by the Human Organ Transplants Act 1989 which regulates transplants between living people of non-regenerative organs[1] only. It is however noteworthy that the 1989 Act does not distinguish between child and adult organ donors, an omission which I consider to be deplorable but also symptomatic of a more general legal apathy towards children used as donors.

What of the case-law approach to child bone-marrow donors? Judicial guidance on transplants of bone-marrow harvested from children has never been sought so no specific precedent is available. Turning to general principles of medical law, two quite distinct approaches have been adopted towards medical interventions involving children.

The first of these permits a medical procedure only if it is in the best interests of the child who undergoes it; in other words, parents can only validly consent to treatment which is in their children's best interests and if they apparently consent to other treatment, their consent should be, if not ignored by medical staff, then at least tested in a court of law. This test governs most medical decision-making for children. Parents and medical staff who fail to act in the best interests of a child lose their legal right to make decisions on behalf of that child. Where a child's carers disagree on what might constitute the best course of action, application should be made to the court.

This approach was endorsed by the House of Lords in *Gillick v West Norfolk and Wisbech Area Health Authority* (1985)[2] It has been applied to therapeutic[3] and non-therapeutic[4] interventions. It is consistent with Children Act 1989 and general child-law principles. There is however no precedent for its adoption in cases in which parents volunteer children for medical treatment meant to help another person.

The second approach accepts that parents can give valid consent to treatments which are 'not against the interests of the child'. It was developed in order to permit the taking of blood samples from children whose legitimacy or parentage were in issue.[5] It has been argued by Skegg[6] that the approach is relevant to any medical intervention carried out on a child for the benefit of another person, whether this be a man seeking to deny his maintenance obligations to a child or the potential recipient of an organ transplant or bone-marrow donation. Judicial authority for the adoption of the approach is limited to blood sampling cases, however, and the recent Court of Appeal Judgment in

---

1   Human Organ Transplants Act 1989 s 7(2).
2   [1985] 3 All ER 402.
3   Eg *Re B* [1981] 1 WLR 1421.
4   Eg *Re B* [1987] 2 All ER 206.
5   *S v S; W v Official Solicitor* [1970] 3 All ER 107.
6   Skegg 'Consent to Medical Procedures on Minors' 36 MLR 370, 381.

the case of *Re F (A Minor: Paternity Test)* (1993)[7] has made it clear that taking a blood sample for DNA profiling may well be against a child's interests if the stability of the family unit in which the child lives is disturbed by the outcome of the medical procedure.

How do these two approaches relate to bone-marrow donations? Assessing whether harvesting bone-marrow is 'in the best interests' of the donor-child or 'not against the interests' of the child must take into account the medical aspects of the intervention. The child will need to undergo tests to check whether his or her bone-marrow is a suitable 'match'. If it is, he or she will be hospitalised for up to two nights and a general anaesthetic will be administered, thus putting the child at some risk of coma, brain damage, even death. The extraction of bone-marrow by hypodermic syringe from the hip-bone will leave at least a sensation of severe discomfort.[8]

Should any factors be set against the negative aspects of the intervention? The use to which the bone-marrow is put may confer psychological benefits: the child may want the bone-marrow recipient to survive and may feel satisfaction at being able to help with that survival. At the very least, the child will bask in the approval of its parents, and of the medical staff who carry out the transplant.

Of course the situation has its psychological dangers: to what extent can the child be persuaded that he or she has an emotional stake in helping the recipient of the bone-marrow? To what extent does he or she fear parental disapproval if he or she fails to co-operate?

Assessments based on factors such as these will not inevitably lead to the conclusion that a donation is 'in the best interests' of the donor. They may, indeed, under the second test, fail even to conclude that the interests of the child will at least not be harmed. Where the proposed child-donor is too young to have established an emotional bond with the proposed recipient of the bone-marrow the factors favouring the medical intervention appear to me outweighed by those against it. It should, however, be noted that in America, donation of skin by a three year old was judged acceptable as being in his interests.[9]

I hope I have shown so far that English law may not approve of medical altruism in children. In view of this it might seem logical that child donor cases should be vetted in court. Whether the law requires this is by no means certain. The 'special category' of medical cases identified by Lord Donaldson in *F v West Berkshire* (1989)[10] at its Court of Appeal stage as needing court referral included organ donation but bone-marrow donation was not mentioned. Although the case concerned a mentally incapacitated adult, the Official Solicitor applies the same 'special category' approach in children

---

7   [1993] 1 FLR 598.

8   Information made available by The Anthony Nolan Bone Marrow Trust, Royal Free Hospital, London NW3 2QG.

9   *McMahon v McMahon* (1963), unreported, discussed by Skegg, op cit n 6 supra at p 378.

10   *Re F (Sterilisation: Mental Patient)* [1989] 2 FLR 376, 390H.

cases.[11] While a policy of non-intervention has its attractions, it must be the case that parents will not inevitably be impartial when bone-marrow donation is considered. If, as was the case for the Ayalas, the life of one child is under serious threat, the urge to 'volunteer' another child may overwhelm the parents.

It has been argued[12] that it is not unethical for parents to inflict some risk on children. Children may be taken on car journeys! But surely such an argument only holds good where the benefits to the child of what causes the risks outweigh the latter. It is precisely this calculation which is so difficult in the context of bone-marrow donation.

How should the law approach the child bone-marrow donor? It should, in my view, aim for consistency with, on the one hand, Children Act philosophy, and, on the other, the proposals of the Law Commission relating to the medical treatment of adults who are mentally incapacitated.[13] It should borrow from the Children Act the willingness to attend to the child's point of view. Given the nature and purpose of bone-marrow harvesting, I would argue that the wishes of the proposed child donor, whatever his or her age might be, should prevail. In order to assess those wishes impartially, some independent forum would be needed. The type of forum mooted by the Law Commission might fit the bill: not a formal court but a tribunal which could play an active part in eliciting relevant information.[14] An independent medical social worker who would interview the child might be a satisfactory alternative.

Situations in which the proposed child donor is too young to voice opinions could be referred to the tribunal. Alternatively the law might provide that such young children should never be volunteered for bone-marrow donation.

Allowing the wishes of the proposed child donor to prevail would seem to be acceptable to the courts. Whatever the shortcomings of Lord Donaldson's judgment in the case of anorexic *Re W* (1992)[15] he did appear to feel that doctors should not act in transplant cases unless the child donor's consent had been obtained.

The legal position should, above all, be clear and one, not two, tests should be understood to govern child bone-marrow donation. That test, again for the sake of consistency, should be the 'is it in the donor's best interests' test.

Surely the young child who might give bone-marrow should have the full protection offered by the law to children generally. No child should be expected by the law to make him or herself available in medical procedures to promote the welfare of another.

---

11 Nicholls, M 'Consent to Medical Treatment' (1993) Fam Law 30.
12 Gillon, R 'Research on the Vulnerable' in *Protecting the Vulnerable* ed Brazier, M (1992) Routledge p 52.
13 The Law Commission, Consultation Paper (1993) No 129 HMSO.
14 The Law Commission op cit n 13 supra para 4.5.
15 [1992] 4 All ER 627, 635.

Chapter 5

Children's Rights in Relation to Giving and Withholding their Consent to Treatment

Maria Ruegger
Bedford College of Higher Education

The 1989 Children Act which came into force on the 14 October 1991, has brought with it many changes, both legal and attitudinal. Since then courts have had to adjudicate in many situations involving ethical and moral dilemmas, one of which concerns the extent of control which courts should exercise over a child's right to give or withhold consent to medical treatment and case law is in the process of being built up.

I will argue that it would be more appropriate for local authorities to use mental health legislation in preference to child care law when there are disputes between young people and their psychiatrists over treatment for mental disorder. This would safeguard rights that all children have obtained as a result of the Children Act 1989, namely the right to make their own decisions about medical treatment when they are considered competent to do so. In addition it would make available to those who need to be detained and treated against their will rights to second opinions and independent reviews that would not be available to them otherwise.

I shall begin by summarising the content of the relevant legislation and examining the impact of recent judicial decisions on children's rights before going on to consider in detail the advantages afforded by the Mental Health Act 1983.

The Children Act embodies radical new thinking about the rights of children to make and/or contribute to decisions that are to be made about their treatment and care. There are five specific provisions in the act[1] that give a child who is judged capable of making an informed decision the right to refuse to submit to medical and psychiatric examinations, and in the case of supervision orders children have been given the power to refuse psychiatric and medical treatment.

The idea that children under 16 years of age could and should be consulted about such matters first found recognition in British Law in 1985 when the House of Lords formulated the basis of a concept now known as 'Gillick

---

1   Sections 38(6), 43(8), 44(7), paras 4(4)(a) and 5(5)(a) of Schedule 3.

competence' in which the ability of a child under 16 to make his own medical decisions is evaluated according to his chronological age, and considered in conjunction with his mental and emotional maturity, intelligence, and comprehension. The case law[2] established on this occasion led to children being given the right to make their own decisions with regard to medical treatment when judged to be of sufficient understanding and intelligence, irrespective of the wishes of their parents.

Children aged 16 and over in fact acquired the right to give and withhold their consent to medical treatment by virtue of the Family Law Reform Act 1969, when the age of majority was lowered from 21 years to 18 years.

The current position then as far as statutory legislation is concerned is as follows:

1   At age 16 children gain the absolute right to give informed consent to surgical, medical, psychiatric and dental treatment (Family Law Reform Act 1969).

2   Under 16-year-olds, if judged to be of 'sufficient understanding to make an informed decision', have the right to give or withhold consent to medical examination and/or treatment (Children Act 1989 s 38(6), s 43(8), s 44(7), paras 4(4) (a) and 5(5)(a) of Schedule 3).

3   Those with parental responsibility for children under 16 who are not considered to be of 'sufficient understanding' to make an informed decision have the right to give and withhold consent on the child's behalf (Children Act 1989 s 3).

But

Recent case law has established that those with parental responsibility, and ultimately the High Court, have the right to overrule decisions made by under 18 year olds, Gillick competent minors, and their parents, should they refuse to give their consent to treatments advised by doctors.

Lord Donaldson in a Court of Appeal decision *Re R* (1992)[3] formed the view that Gillick competent minors shared the right to give or withhold consent with their parents, and that only a refusal by all three would create a veto on proposed treatment. In the case of *Re R*, a 15-year-old girl was refusing medication for a psychotic condition. This case was decided prior to the Children Act coming into force but Lord Donaldson reached similar

---

2   [1986] AC 112. (Mrs Gillick, requested of the Health Authority that her daughters not be given contraceptive advice whilst under 16 years without her expressed consent. The House of Lords ruled that parental rights yielded to a child's right to make decisions about medical treatment when the child was judged competent so to do.)

3   [1991] 4 All ER 177; [1992] 1 FLR 190.

conclusions in a later case *Re W* (1992)[4] concerning a 16-year-old who was refusing treatment for anorexia nervosa. Again this child was judged 'Gillick Competent', and the rationale for overriding her refusal to accept treatment was based on s 8(3) of the Family Law Reform Act which states that 'Nothing in this section shall be construed as making ineffective any consent which would have been effective if this section had not been enacted'. Lord Donaldson took the view that this implied that these pre-existing rights belonged to those with parental responsibilities, although authorities such as Hoggett,[5] Bromley,[6] and Freeman,[7] would disagree with this interpretation, and hence case law has established the principle that 'Gillick competent' children can be treated against their will if both, or either of their parents, or any other person or body with parental responsibility, give their consent. As Michael Freeman points out this will 'remove autonomy and self determination from children at an age when more responsibility and self direction is expected of them,[8] and is contrary to the general philosophy enshrined in the Gillick judgment and the Children Act 1989, which emphasises the empowering of children to participate as much as they are able to in decisions about themselves. It also will deprive most of those likely to be affected by these judgments of rights that they could have by virtue of the Mental Health Act 1983, namely the right to second opinions in disputes about treatment, and access to Mental Health Review Tribunals to put their case for discharge from detention.

In the cases of both *Re R* and *Re W* the actions of the local authority in seeking the inherent jurisdiction of the High Court rather than using the 1983 Mental Health Act raises fundamental issues concerned with attitudes towards the rights of young people to be involved and consulted about decisions that effect them. For example, W was 16-years-old and, in the opinion of the local authority, required treatment, against her wishes if necessary,in a psychiatric hospital specialising in the treatment of eating disorders such as anorexia nervosa. It is not uncommon for those under and over 16 years of age with the same condition as W who are refusing treatment, to be compulsorily admitted to hospital and treated against their will if two doctors, one of whom must have recognised special expertise in psychiatry, and an approved social worker who has undertaken specialist training in this field, judge that the criteria under s 2 or s 3 of the Mental Health Act 1983 are satisfied. The grounds to be satisfied are as follows:

---

4   [1992] 4 All ER 627.

5   *Parents and Children* (1981) p 12 Sweet and Maxwell, London.

6   *Family Law* (1987) p 275 Butterworths, London.

7   Freeman, M 'Removing rights from adolescents' *Adoption and Fostering* (1993) 17, 1: 14-19.

8   Ibid.

1   That there is evidence of mental disorder (s 2) or mental illness
       (s 3) and that this cannot be treated unless the patient is detained
       under this section; and

2   That it is in the interests of the patients health and safety for her
       to be detained.

Even when the decision is that the grounds are satisfied, the patient has the
right to have their case heard by a Mental Health Review Tribunal within 14
days if detained on a s 2, and once in every six month period if detained on a
s 3.[9] Patients detained under section must have their informed consent sought
for treatments that are proposed. Although medication can be given against
the patients' wishes for a period of three months, at the expiration of this
period they acquire the right to a second opinion from an independent expert
appointed by the Mental Health Act Commission.[10] Rights to independent
opinions in relation to refusal to consent to the administration of electro-
convulsive therapy are acquired on admission, and without the three month
delay that applies to the administration of medication,[11] although there are
powers to enable doctors to act in emergencies if it is felt that not to do so
would seriously endanger the health of the patient.[12]

In addition, the patient's nearest relative acquires rights to information
about their detention and care,[13] the power of veto in relation to an application
for admission for treatment (s 3),[14] the right to discharge the patient subject
only to the responsible medical officer's refusal on the single ground that the
patient if discharged would be likely to act in a manner dangerous to himself
or others,[15] and the right to appoint an independent medical practitioner for
the purpose of advising them whether to exercise their right to discharge the
patient.[16]

One wonders why the local authority chose to seek the inherent
jurisdiction of the High Court in wardship in preference to mental health
legislation in relation to young people thought to be suffering from mental
disorder. It seems to me that there are four distinct advantages in having
resource to Mental Health Law.

First and perhaps the most obvious benefit is the rights to information,
reviews, and second opinions that are acquired in relation to both detention
and treatment.

---

9   Section 66, Mental Health Act 1983.
10 Section 58(1)(b) Mental Health Act 1983.
11 Section 58(1)(a) Mental Health Act 1983.
12 Section 62 Mental Health Act 1983.
13 See for example, s 11(3), s 133.
14 Section11(4).
15 Sections 23 and 25.
16 Section 24.

Secondly, there are no age criteria to be concerned with. There is no minimum age in the Mental Health Act. It is thus possible to consider each case on its own merits by keeping the focus solely on whether there is evidence of mental disorder, and if so whether this is so serious as to require detention and/or treatment against the person's will, in the opinion of those who are experts in this area.

Thirdly, to use mental health legislation avoids the possibility of young people being subjected to 'backdoor' admissions organised by those with parental responsibility in situations where the criteria for detention under mental health legislation would not be met.

Fourthly, if it were the case that young people were only deprived of the right to make their own decisions about medical treatment on grounds of mental disorder then this would clearly leave decisions about all other treatments, for example sterilisations, abortions etc, with those for whom the treatment is proposed. This would then mean that courts would only be involved in cases where it was clear that the person, (adult or child), is not competent and will never be, as is the case with those who have a severe learning disability. There would then be no question of young people thought competent enough to make their own decisions having treatments forced upon them.

I would now like to consider in greater detail some of the practice issues raised by the preference shown by local authorities for the use of child care law as opposed to mental health law when dealing with young people who have a mental disorder. In my view this constitutes an unwarranted intrusion into the lives of others and is a departure from the usual way of responding to young people in the process of acquiring the legal rights and social responsibilities associated with full adult status. For example young people of sixteen can choose whether to stay on at school or to take up full time employment, they can request that they be accommodated by the local authority or admitted to a psychiatric hospital in their own right, those who have been in care are being assisted by their social workers in acquiring both the skills necessary for independent living and the resources to enable them to do so. Had the local authorities concerned in *Re R* and *Re W* invoked mental health legislation rather than the powers of the High Court, this would have been in line with their more usual practice of recognising that children of 15 and 16 years of age are at least as likely as adults to make reasonable decisions about what is in their best interests. The young people concerned would then only have been deprived of their right to decide for themselves whether the proposed treatments were worse than their conditions if they were judged to be suffering from a mental disorder serious enough to warrant over-riding their own wishes.

It is clear from current literature on social work practice with young people that it is not the norm for local authorities sharing parental rights to take an authoritarian view of their role. In my experience as a guardian *ad litem* the reverse is more often the case in that a young person's views on major decisions affecting them are not only sought, but listened to and respected. In cases where there are disagreements between youngsters and their carers great efforts are made to resolve these in a way which respects the child's integrity and right to their opinion, frequently involving the appointing of an independent advisor or advocate for the child to enable them to represent their views effectively at decision making meetings. There appears to be a willingness to compromise and to listen together with an avoidance of the 'we know what is best for you' stance in current social work practice that does not extend to those thought to be suffering from mental disorder.

Since *Re R* and *Re W* there has been an increasing trend in local authorities of involving the courts when decisions about treatment for mental disorder have had to be made. In one such case[17] a local authority applied for care proceedings on the grounds that a 'Gillick competent' child who was refusing to submit to assessment and psychiatric examination and treatment at an adolescent unit, was beyond the control of her parent. The authority then successfully invoked the court's powers in wardship to override the child's refusal to comply with an order made under s 38(6) requiring her to receive examination and if necessary treatment. Was this an attempt to obtain a backdoor admission in a situation where it was feared the criteria for compulsory admission under the Mental Health Act would not have been met?

There is now a danger that it will become common practice for local authorities to apply for specific issue orders before admitting children to adolescent units following the decision in *Re K, W and H* (1993)[18], which was concerned with applications made in respect of three young people who were to be admitted to units within St Andrews Psychiatric Hospital specialising in the treatment of highly disturbed adolescents. These applications were made in response to a health authority report which recommended that s 8 orders should be sought authorising the treatment of children in the units, and in my view probably reflects confusion amongst medical staff as regards who they should look to for a valid consent together with the need to cover themselves.

Another even more worrying case concerns the Court of Appeal's refusal to grant a young woman judicial review of the local authority's decision to place her for assessment as a 'voluntary' patient in a psychiatric hospital against her will.[19]

Should not local authorities have enabled all of these young people to have their situations assessed under mental health legislation by people

---

17   *South Glamorgan CC v B* [1993] 1 FCR 626; [1993] 1 FLR 574.
18   *Re K, W and H (Minors) (Consent to Treatments)* (1993) 1 FCR 240.
19   *R v Kirklees Metropolitian Council ex p C (A Minor)* (1993) *The Times* 25 March.

knowledgeable about the conditions from which they are suffering? To have done so would have been in accord with the legal principles laid down in the Gillick judgment, The Family Law Reform Act 1969, The Children Act 1989, and the recent International Convention on the Rights of Children. In addition it would accord rights-conscious adolescents the built in safeguards and rights of appeal available under mental health legislation, and hence the sense hopefully of being treated fairly in a manner which reflects the ways in which they have been taught to expect that they will be treated, that is with dignity and respect in recognition of their approaching adulthood. Instead, by invoking the powers of the courts, these adolescents have been in effect treated like very young children in that they have been forced to submit to medical treatment decided upon by others who consider they know best, with no subsequent right of appeal or other opportunity to be heard.

Conclusion

The case law that has been established as a result of *Re R* and *Re W*, the case brought by St Andrews, and the Kirklees case, effectively deprives all 'Gillick competent' children under the age of 16 of the rights they have so recently acquired under the 1989 Children Act, and all 16 to 18 year olds of the rights they have had since the passing of the Family Law Reform Act in 1969, to give or withhold their consent to medical examinations and treatment irrespective of the wishes of their parents or guardians. An example offered by Michael Freeman illustrates the ludicrous situation that now exists in English Law. A 17-year-old could be forced to undergo an abortion against her wishes should anyone with parental responsibility for her give their consent, yet that same seventeen year old, if she had her child, would have more control over decisions relating to her baby that to those concerning her own body.

When one considers that young people are likely to learn much more about parenting from how they themselves are treated than any other source, can we really say we are offering them a sound model on which to build their own parenting skills? The current model is full of contradictions since on the one hand it preaches about their rights to self determination, to be listened to, and to have their views heard and respected, yet in practice adopts an authoritarian 'you will do as I say as far as decisions about your body are concerned' approach. Hopefully some adolescents will be brave enough, if given appropriate help and support from those on whom they depend, to challenge this case law that represents a judicial backlash aimed at limiting their autonomy. For most, if not all, of those for whom this is not judged to be an appropriate course of action, then use of the Mental Health Act 1983 provides an alternative which goes considerably further than case law in treating 'Gillick competent' minors in a humane manner consistent with the philosophy and principles on which current child care practice is based.

Chapter 6

Joint Parenting Under The Children Act 1989

Christine Piper & Felicity Kaganas
Brunel University

'Parental responsibility' has become a much referred to concept, used in many different circumstances to convey a multiplicity of ideas and norms.[1] This paper will focus, however, solely on the concept of parental responsibility as a mechanism for preserving parental status in the face of family breakdown. The solution of joint but independent parenting adopted in the Children Act of 1989[2] emerged as a response to the criticisms of the previous legal framework. The 1989 Act ostensibly provides a new and quite different set of legal principles and processes for determining the allocation of the 'rights, duties, powers, responsibilities and authority' of parents.

The main problem bedevilling the pre-1989 law were highlighted by the Law Commission in its deliberations over reform. Amongst them were difficulties stemming from the lack of uniformity in the orders available. This confusion was exacerbated by the lack of uniformity among courts reflected in geographical differences in the use of the available orders. For example, while joint custody remained rare nationally during the 1980s, it was found in a study of ten courts that it was more prevalent in the south of England than in the north of the country.[3] This study also indicated that sole custody (rather than split custody) predominated. Another major concern, and the one on which this paper will focus, was that the effects of the various orders were not clear.[4]

Until *Dipper v Dipper* (1981)[5] it was assumed that a sole custody or a split order gave all the decision-making power to the custodial parent. However, in *Dipper* it was stated that, 'The parent is always entitled, whatever his custodial status, to know and be consulted about the future education of the children and any other major matters'.[6] Yet what qualified as 'major' in this context was not comprehensively defined. Similarly, it was not clear what

---

1   For a discussion in the context of divorce mediation see Piper, C *The Responsible Parent* (1993) Harvester Wheatsheaf.

2   Children Act 1989 ss 2 and 3.

3   See Hoggett, B and Pearl, D *The Family, Law and Society: Cases and Materials* Butterworths 504-6.

4   Law Commission No 172 *Family Law, Review of Child Care Law, Guardianship and Custody* (1988) HMSO para 4.

5   (1981) Fam Law 31.

6   At 48.

powers and responsibilities a joint custody order gave each parent. It was clear that, in terms of s 1(1) of the Guardianship Act 1973, neither parent could act against the wishes of the other[7] and in that sense each parent could veto the plans of the other. However, the scope of this veto remained unclear. It was accepted that it did not extend to the sphere of care and control but the limits of this area had never been defined.[8] Under the Domestic Proceedings and Magistrates Court Act 1978 and the Guardianship of Minors Act 1971, the sharing of legal custody was also possible but, again, statute and case law had not clarified the precise effect of the order.[9]

All the available orders therefore involved problems of indeterminacy - problems which could have been addressed within the existing framework. However, this framework had been subjected to severe and growing criticism. A comprehensive revision of the law was called for. Sole custody was seen to exclude one parent and was increasingly portrayed as 'bad' for the child. Detractors of joint custody, on the other hand, pointed out that, by imposing co-operation, it was impractical and undermined the interests of the caretaking mother.

Despite the chorus of objections to joint custody, it continued to be advocated as the preferred arrangement to promote the welfare of children. In the early and mid 1980s there emerged a body of literature by academics, practitioners and feminist groups expressing alarm at the joint custody provisions being adopted in some jurisdictions. In 1982, for example, Schulman argued that joint custody was less a triumph for child welfare than a victory for the father's rights movement.[10] Research was somewhat fragmented but Steinman concluded, in 1983, that 'the evidence we currently have does not support a legal presumption in favour of joint custody' and that:

'We cannot expect a court order of joint custody to create co-operative parenting ... Joint custody from a legal point of view does not automatically become joint custody from the psychological point of view.'[11]

A decade later, the issue is still controversial. Recent criticism had focused on the potential of joint custody to provide fathers with a source of continuing power through the assumption of parity with the caretaking mother in decision-making after divorce.[12] The existence of legal mechanisms for

7   Section 1(1) Guardianship Act 1973.
8   The Law Commission, Working Paper No 96, *Family Law, Review of Child Law: Custody* (1986) para 2.38 HMSO.
9   Working Paper No 96 para 2.47.
10 Schulman, J in *The Women's Advocate* Vol 3 No 2 pp 3 and 6.
11 *Davis U C Law Review* (1983) Vol 16, 739-62 at pp 758 and 759 respectively.
12 Holtrust, Nora, Sevenhuijsen, Selma and Verbraken, Annick 'Right for Fathers and the State: Recent Developments in Custody Politics in the Netherlands' in *Child Custody and the Politics of Gender*, Smart, Carol and Sevenhuijsen, Selma (eds) (1989) Routledge 51, 65.

challenging mothers' decisions may lead to increased litigation and has prompted the argument that co-operative parenting will be undermined rather than strengthened if litigation proliferates.

Indeed, the prospect of parental conflict led courts in several jurisdictions to award joint custody sparingly. For example, whilst most American states have endorsed joint custody, it is not considered appropriate in all cases. A survey conducted in Michigan of the views of judges there revealed that they believed joint custody to be appropriate in cases where both parents appeared equally worthy, but at least half of the judges were reluctant to make such an order if neither parent wanted it.[13] More recently, academics in several countries have been concerned at the prospect of joint custody ordered by the court or sanctioned by in-court mediation where there is a history of domestic violence or child abuse[14]. In California the presumption in favour of joint custody has been removed from the statute book because of general concern about joint custody in practice.[15]

It is perhaps surprising, that the Children Act has constructed a legal form of joint parenting that amounts to a presumption of joint custody.[16] This legal framework is, on the face of it, very different from that obtaining under the previous law. As the Law Commission recommended,[17] parents now have equal status. The mother and the father can act independently of each other unless a court order is in force to restrict particular aspects of responsibility. For the first fifteen months of the Act's operation it was assumed the Act did not impose a duty on parents to consult with each other. However, some uncertainty has been created by the statement by Glidewell LJ in *Re G* that, in the context of a child's schooling, a non-caretaking mother with parental responsibility was entitled to be consulted.[18] Nevertheless, there does appear to be one clear change in that, where there is a disagreement, the burden of initiating proceedings to resolve a dispute now rests with the absent parent who must make an application for a s 8 order. This contrasts with the *de facto* veto of an absent parent when joint custody was awarded.[19]

Both parents therefore have equal decision-making powers in relation to their children. If the Children Act is operating as envisaged, then the preservation of parental status after divorce through the legal concept of

13 Smith, E Craig 'Joint Custody: The View from the Bench' (1984) 63 Michigan Bar Journal at 1551-5.

14 See, for example, Berns, Sandra S 'Living Under the Shadow of Rousseau: The Role of Gender Ideologies in Custody and Access Decisions' (1991) 10 *U of Tasmania L Rev* 233, 254 and Astor, Hilary 'Doing the Impossible: Talking About Violence in Family Mediation', unpublished paper, Sydney University.

15 Cal Civ Code S 4600(d) (West Supp 1989).

16 See John Dewar *Law and the Family* (2nd ed), Butterworths at 355.

17 Report No 172 para 4.5.

18 *Re G (A Minor)* (1993) 5 January, Lexis Transcript.

19 Under s 1(3) Guardianship Act 1973.

'parental responsibility' should be encouraging co-operation. By removing the possibility of the courts awarding one parent the 'total package' of sole custody[20] it should have lowered the stakes and reduced the bitterness and conflict that present obstacles to co-operative parenting. Alternatively, by giving the ever 'responsible' parent wider powers to intervene, it may have increased conflict; parents have been provided with more opportunities to 'legalise' their disputes.[21] Firstly, wardship, the primary mechanism for resolving disputes before the 1989 Act, was a cumbersome and costly procedure whereas a prohibited steps order or a specific issue order can be obtained by a much simpler procedure. Secondly, the scope of s 8 orders is left wide open in the Children Act; they are not limited to the 'major' decisions referred to in *Dipper* or to what the Law Commission called the 'strategic' decisions which should have been shared under a joint custody order.[22]

The Act has been in operation for only two years and that is a relatively short period of time in which to collect valid evidence and draw conclusions about new parenting patterns. However, it is worth examining briefly data available from two sources in the UK for indications of possible developments. The first source is case law from the Appeal Court and the Family division, the second is statistical data from the Lord Chancellor's Department on s 8 orders being made in Family Proceedings courts.[23]

The first source - reported cases (including Lexis transcripts) - indicates a paucity of intra-familial applications for specific issue and prohibited steps orders. Our research uncovered only 13 private law cases in which either order, or a combination of both, was applied for, with reports for a further 13 cases in which there was evidence that prohibited steps and specific issue orders had been awarded or applied for previously. Not only was the number of cases smaller than might have been expected, reported cases also suggest that the issues disputed were clearly akin to those which were disputed before the implementation of the Children Act. For example, one case concerned the sterilisation of a young woman, aged almost 18, suffering from severe epilepsy and a chromosomal deficiency;[24] three cases involved a dispute over which school the children should attend; and one case involved a dispute about a change of name. However, with 15 cases in this small sample focusing

---

20 See, for example, King, M 'Playing the Symbols: Custody and the Law Commission' (1987) *Family Law* Vol 17, 186-91.

21 See Dewar op cit p 356.

22 Working Paper No 96 para 4.39.

23 In addition the Children Act Advisory Committee, based in the LCD, and the Law Society's Legal Practice Directorate are monitoring the operation of the Act.

24 *Re HG (Specific Issue Order: Sterilisation)* [1993] 1 FLR 587. It has since been confirmed in a Practice Note that proceedings to authorise the sterilisation of a minor may take the form of an application for a specific issue order. However the preferred course is an application under the inherent jurisdiction: *Practice Note* [1993] 3 All ER 222.

on the removal or anticipated removal of children either from a parent or from the jurisdiction, this major and 'one-off' decision is still dominating the litigation.

It would appear that the courts are not being used by parents to settle disputes over 'minor' issues or over the details of child-care arrangements. This conclusion is supported by statistics collected and made available by the Lord Chancellor's Department. Between October 1991 and June 1992 only about 5,000 applications for prohibited steps orders and about 2,000 for specific issue orders were made.[25] This compares with a much larger number of 20,000 applications for contact orders in the same period.

There are a number of possible explanations for these findings. One is that there is now a greater incidence of joint parenting. This assumes that the evidence indicates that disputes are not occurring or they are quickly settled within the family. It could be that discussions prior to the Act and the considerable publicity surrounding the implementation of the Act have led to an ideological change; expectations of what post-separation parenting entails are now different. In addition, the normative message that parents should co-operate has led to greater actual co-operation.

An alternative explanation might be that joint parenting does continue after separation and divorce but that it is a continuation of segregated roles.[26] A recent survey[27] found that fathers were not equal partners in the provision of child care. More than 80% of the parents surveyed said that mothers were still usually responsible for the basic essentials of food, clothes and health care in the family and even in the sphere of education about 50% still apportioned primary responsibility to the mother. The large number of contact, as opposed to specific issue and prohibited steps orders, might suggest that fathers want no more involvement in parenting than regular contact with their children.

It may be, however, that there are more separated parents than the evidence would suggest who are *not* experiencing consensual joint parenting, whether or not the non-resident parent is an active or passive partner in this enterprise. There may be disputes between parents and parents may want these disputes settled but they are not using the new legal procedures to do so. This clearly raises the question of why s 8 orders are not in practice used or available even when there is an acknowledged dispute.

One answer might be, borrowing from the feminist critique of joint custody, that mothers, for whatever reason, may be deferring to the father's wish to contribute to decision-making. However, a second set of answers is required if one assumes that parents do want to use the law but are being diverted away from the courts. It may be that professionals, notably solicitors

---

25 The Children Act Advisory Committee Annual Report 1991-2 Table 3 p 40.

26 See, for example Bott, Elizabeth *Family and Social Networks* (1957) London: Tavistock.

27 'Home Truths' Focus *The Sunday Times* 29 August 1993.

who are still the most frequent 'first stop' for disputing couples, are not
advising the use of s 8 applications, either because of a belief in private
ordering as the best form of dispute resolution or because of a lack of
knowledge about the intended scope of the new legal rules. Linked to this
could be a trend towards the diversion of disputing parents to mediation by
solicitors, divorce court welfare officers and judges themselves. Lastly, there
is the possibility that parents are making s 8 applications but that the
interpretation and operation of the non-intervention principle contained in the
Children Act is leading to a situation where few orders are made.

As yet little research has been done in the UK to illuminate the statistics.[28]
Research conducted in California suggests that the capacity of family law to
effect behavioural change is very limited.[29] Maccoby and Mnookin point out
that traditional gender roles predominate in marriage[30] and that this pattern
persists after divorce.[31] In short, 'the characteristic roles of mothers and
fathers remain fundamentally different'.[32] In their large sample of Californian
families, they found that joint legal custody orders had no significant effects
on contact, support or involvement in decision-making. Only about 30% of
their sample were able to establish co-operative parenting relationships.[33] The
most common pattern was characterised by spousal disengagement which
involved 'parallel parenting'.[34] There was little communication between the
parents, who avoided each other, and each established an independent child-
care routine. This meant that the parent with whom the children resided had
considerably more information about, and control over, their upbringing.
There was little consultation and then over major issues only.[35] Many
indicated, therefore, that in some ways it was easier to raise their children in
accordance with their own values, 'with less need to consider those of the
other parent'.[36] The authors conclude that, 'After separation, there appears to
be no way in which a parent can truly have a voice in what is happening to the
children in the other household'.[37]

In the light of this study, it seems possible that English parents too are
'disengaged' and that the caretaking parent makes decisions of which the

---

28 See, however, the report of the research done by Demetra Pappas: 'Direction or Conciliation: The
    Theory and Reality of Preliminary Hearings Conducted at Croydon, England, Under the Children
    Act 1989' *Family and Conciliation Courts Review* (1993) Vol 31, No 3, 327-353.
29 Maccoby, E and Mnookin, R *Dividing the Child: Social and Legal Dilemmas of Custody* (1992)
    Harvard University Press at 286.
30 Ibid at 26.
31 Ibid at 267-9 and 271.
32 Ibid at 271.
33 Ibid at 272.
34 Ibid at 277.
35 Ibid at 219.
36 Ibid at 278.
37 Ibid at 295.

other parent is not even aware. The absence of litigation over the details of child care might stem from genuine ignorance and lack of communication rather than from the exercise of co-operative relationships between parents. The research we are currently planning hopes to address these possibilities and provide a clearer picture.

Chapter 7

The Children Act and Day Care for Young Children: The Market Economy of Legal Control

Ian Mallinson
Moray House Institute
Heriot Watt University

Abstract

Department of Health circular LAC(93)1 published in January 1993 'reinterpreted' the standards to be applied in inspection and registration of day dare of young children. The Government, it could be argued, responded to fears of potential public outcry as much as to the question of whether the standards previously set, were too high. Controls were said in the media to be expensive, petty and rigorous. Whilst evidence justifying cancellation of registration would have to stand up in court, it was clear that the economic costs of requirements designed to safeguard the welfare of children was a factor that would cause many small businesses to fold. Changes have now been placed on top of the pre-existing guidance. As a result, the legal framework can no longer be said to be 'cut and dried'. Implementation presumes philosophy and at street level, aims that were said to have become skewed have now undergone a further twist. Presumptions under the legislation were and still are unclear. Local needs and national concerns mixed together in variable quantities are a murky brew. Crucial issues such as who are fit persons and what are safety standards may now have to be decided by precedents yet to be set in the courts. 'Reinterpretation' rather than a clear restatement of purpose and a firm redefining of guidance does not solve the dilemmas of the registration officer. The standards to be applied now have to be further debated at local level. Nationally, tinkering with markets rather than re-establishing clarity in standards and purpose may be said to derive from political and legal expediency.

Introduction

In the years 1985 to 1988 private and voluntary day care expanded by 44% in England (30% in Wales) whilst child minding increased by 30% throughout the UK (Cohen 1990 pp 19-21; Moss 1991). According to Pugh (1988) 'the registration process is the key to the maintenance and improvement of standards' (p 88) yet Freeman (1992) maintained that under the old 1948 Act this was 'the most unregulated form of substitute care. The registration system has not thought to have been very effective' (p 215). The 1989 Children Act sought to strengthen controls as the brave new world of high quality child care was to be achieved nationally. In the forward to a survey commissioned to develop practice requirements for the 1989 Act (Elfer and Beasley 1991) Virginia Bottomley expressed the essential need for proper regulation to ensure standards. The authors state that it was generally 'accepted that the wide variations in the interpretation of 'fitness' (under the 1948 Act) and the lack of specific requirements ... contributed to considerable difficulties in enforcing minimum standards of care.' The guidance for day care under the 1989 Act (Department of Health; 1991) was thus required 'to protect children, to provide reassurance (to the service user) ... to ensure services meet acceptable standards ... (and) to ensure that people wishing to provide services for children do so within an agreed framework' (para 4.9). Placed against the backdrop of expansion of private and voluntary day care and child minding, the guidance in acknowledging the development of the service, whilst at the same time being able to insist upon improved standards, was the high point of the registration officer's role.

Department of Health LAC(93)1 published in January 1993 then 'reinterpreted' the standards to be applied in inspection and registration of day care of young children.

First of all, small number of areas were redefined. These may be seen as relatively uncontentious changes. These were:

1   a reduction in the mandatory requirements for sanitary facilities for play groups and day nurseries;

2   exempting childminders from having to register their premises under the Food Premises (Registration) Regulations 1991;

3   additional guidance for home play groups;

4   clarification of day care services in NHS hospitals and the issue of crown immunity.

On the other hand, the circular 'reinterpreted' other areas. These we may see as contentious, not so much in terms of redefinition of standards, but as a problematic methodology. Backtracking on previous statements whilst not retracting them, can do nothing other than give rise to confusion and to misinterpretation.

The introduction to the circular summarised the overall changes involved, and the Department's reasons for these:

'The government is concerned to encourage the expansion of day care facilities of an acceptable standard;

there is a presumption under the legislation that registration should be granted unless there is some good reason why not to do;

guidance issued by the Department does not prescribe legally required standards for registration. It draws attention to factors that need to be considered and offers points of reference;

local authorities should be informed by their perception of local needs as well as by the Department's guidance;

the Department's guidance has been applied over-strictly by some local authorities and a number appear to have insisted on even higher standards without jurisdiction.'

It is this mixture of national and local aims, economic and political objectives that this paper is to examine. Of crucial importance to practice is how they emerge as legal points for the registration officer in their day to day task. The question of the clarity (or otherwise) of the base for regulation is a major issue here.

A question of over regulation?

The issue of Children Act News for February 1993, (Voluntary Organisations Liaison Council for Under Fives 1993) stated the message of the circular: that 'Local Authorities should apply skilled judgment rather than excessive regulation when carrying out ... registration'.

The circular was said to have been 'issued following over 300 complaints to MPs that a number of local authorities were applying the Department's guidance 'over strictly' and insisting upon even higher standards without justification.' The view of the Secretary of State was said to be that 'standards should not be unrealistically high to the point where they inhibit the expansion of day care and childminding services.'

The Children Act Report 1992 (Department of Health and Welsh Office 1993) indicates that many authorities had problems in meeting their numerical targets for registration of day care under the new requirements. The aspects of over zealous registration standards said in the report to give rise to particular difficulties (on examination of the MP's correspondence) were: application of space standards and child/staff ratios, availability of separate sanitary facilities in day nurseries, proportions of trained staff, registration requirements for people providing playgroups on domestic premises, legislation on food and fire safety, first aid, health checks on applicants, criminal record checks, and definition of supervised activities.

Cranston (1985) suggests that in most situations concerning the use of the law for the purposes of regulation, politicians are generally indifferent to the nuts and bolts of compliance. They generally regard their responsibilities complete once legislation is enacted. Public pressure of the type reflected in the Report, it could be argued, is more about the political process and political objectives rather than what is strictly a concern about the operation of the law.

The facility of departmental research, analysis and evaluation with reports to Parliament indicates that the ground rules for implementation of the law may now have changed since Cranston wrote nearly 10 years ago. That is interesting in itself, in setting the contemporary context of the law and its implementation.

The application of child/staff ratios was highlighted in research in the Children Act Report as a particular issue:

> 'For full day care the variation in ratios (in England) was ... marked particularly for the 2-3 and 3-5 age groups and applied across all types of authority. Twenty-six applied higher ratios (that is fewer children to staff) for the 3-5 age group. For the 2-3 age group 4 authorities have adopted higher ratios and 17 authorities have adopted lower ratios.'

In sessional day care a greater uniformity of recommended ratios was found although a number of shire authorities were reported as using higher ratios for three to five year olds.

All this was in contrast to child minding where, a very high proportion of authorities were using the recommended ratios and there was little variation across the age groups:

> 'Where other ratios have been adopted these were lower than recommended (that is more children to childminders) and were confined primarily to a few shire and metropolitan authorities in the 5-7 and 0-8 range.'

Broadly similar results appeared to exist in the Welsh local authorities.

Previously however Melhuish (1991) in reviewing research on day care in Britain had stated that:

> '... there were some marked differences between public and private sector provision. Private sector nurseries had staff with lower level of training and qualifications and also a markedly worse staff:child ratio.'

The question of having to operate with dual standards has been a difficult one for registration officers.

The conclusions of this part the Children Act Report were however clear:

> 'Some local authorities appeared to have adopted an over-rigid approach to registration of existing provision. As a result many day care providers and child minders were finding it difficult and onerous to comply with the registration requirements imposed by local authorities.'

Political pressure

The Government it could be argued in circular LAC(93)1 responded to fears of potential public outcry as much as to the question of whether the standards previously set were too high. Logically if the previous standards constituted sound child care but were being over interpreted, their restatement rather than reinterpretation would be in order.

The Government had been criticised in the press before the 1989 Act was implemented for not acting firmly to provide a proper nursery service. A leading article in the Independent on 23 September 1991 made the point that the Government left child care provision to 'erratic companies, local councils and individual market decisions made by parents'. The response to a article in the same issue (Jones 1991), that made comparisons with Denmark, provoked a series of letters saying how policy in this country was wrong. Amongst these was a letter (Deech 1991) which demanded a repeal of the regulations and guidance on the control of day care. These regulations were at the time due to be implemented a week later:

'Where the requirement was one member of staff for every six toddlers, an additional full time supervisor is now required where there are 12 children and is not counted in the ratio; where once 30 square foot per baby was demanded it is now 40 and so on. A nappy macerator at a cost of £1000 and 10 cubic foot fridge are specified for 12 toddlers ... Any mother will tell you that you do not need all of this, or seven full time staff to care for 24 toddlers as is now the rule. The effect is to add £25 per week per child to the fee, putting it beyond all but the best paid mothers. The needs of babies and children have not changed over the years; so why are the local authority making these stringent and expensive new rules?'

The authority concerned was merely carrying out the instructions of the Department of Health. Ratios and space requirements were appropriate to fulfil the guidance; for example, the risks to babies lives if a fire occurred and there were not adequate staff to evacuate them, could not be ignored.

Controls when the Act was fully in force were said in the media to be expensive, petty and rigorous. One example is a *Daily Telegraph* report dated 29 October 1992, which inaccurately attributes the change to a transfer of responsibilities from education departments (who had 'not bothered proprietors for 30 years') to social service departments under the Children Act. Under the headline 'Mind your toys, the inspectors are here' the reporter quotes individual instances, summarises the effect of control and in doing so illustrates the dilemmas of the registration officer:

'Nothing from the contents of their toy boxes to their plumbing, is safe from the social services inspectors who are policing the Act. Demands for more staff, the segregation of two and three-year-olds, grandiose kitchen facilities, bigger playrooms, new training courses for staff and additional equipment are gradually squeezing out schools and playgroups for under fives'.

In one case reported to be speaking for thousands of 'teachers' (sic):

'I lose all autonomy, freedom and the ability to grow. Previously I was registered for 60 children. Now I am reduced to 40. I had flexibility and could take children for as little as two or three days, depending upon what their mothers could afford. With the 40 restriction I must fill every place, every day, to get by ... Two of my buildings are purpose built to take 25 children. Now I am limited to 14 each, creating an empty, unfriendly atmosphere ...'.

'... I have stopped taking under-threes because the new ratio represents an increase of 150 per cent on the wages bill which is lunatic ...'.

This required ratio reported in this instance as being 'lunatic' (one to four for under threes) was in fact exactly that which is contained in the guidance. (As was the other ratio quoted; one to eight for three- to five-year-olds). The local authority was simply applying the guidance as it was required too. The Department of Health presumably would, if asked, not quibble with this nor seek to continue the establishment's reported previous lower (and cheaper) ratio of one to ten for all ages! The owner of this day nursery appears here to take issue with the original guidance rather than overzealous interpretation.

She continues:

'(I) ... resent being told how to keep a register, greet parents and organise ... first aid ... Instead of a jug of water for children to wash their hands (I) ... must have hot and cold running water with thermostatically-controlled taps. ... (My) ... tiny pond must be filled in ...'.

It could of course be argued that there was good reason for this. No doubt health and safety inspectors would have been equally concerned about the hazard of the pond as were the social services department.

She then states cynically:

'I did not have enough black dolls (the approved kind have fuzzy hair and thick lips) or puzzles featuring black children. Even the toilet rolls (with holders) were the subject of petty legislation. This school, which I have run for 25 years ceases to be mine. I own the property only. I am emasculated. Eventually I will close.'

The view was put forward by reporter Elizabeth Grice that:

'Schools (sic) will wither as they increase their fees to a level that would keep them viable, but which families cannot afford. As there are no alternative places, mothers will cease to work and there will be real hardship.'

It is interesting that the same paper is now running a similar campaign against 'over zealous social workers' in their inspections of independent boarding schools under the 1989 Act.[1] Exactly the same factors are invoked, ie over regulation resulting in possible closures.

---

1   See for example Jonas, George in the *Daily Telegraph* (1993) 2 June 'Social workers told to curtail checks on private schools', and Marston, Paul (1993) 3 June 'Head who had a basinful'.

The responsibilities and dilemmas of the Local Authority

The Department of Health indicated in the original guidance that local authorities should ensure that the evidence produced to justify cancellation would stand up in court. (The guidance stated in para 7.52 that they should always obtain the advice of their legal department and sought to indicate some of the factors that may be taken into account). Earlier reports (Elfer and Beasley 1991) had suggested that the relationship with the legal department might be about 'the balance that should be struck between giving providers of care the opportunity to improve standards and the duty of the local authority to ensure minimum standards to protect children.' This has a slightly different ring to it!

The framework in the act is clear and stringent in relation to the local authorities' responsibilities. For example, s 73 says that they shall impose *reasonable requirements* on persons seeking registration to provide day care:

1 specifying the maximum numbers, or the maximum number of children within specified age groups, who may be looked after on the premises;

2 requiring the security, maintenance and safety of the premises and equipment;

3 requiring notice of any change in facilities provided or in the period in which they are provided;

4 specifying the number of persons required to assist in looking after children on the premises;

5 requiring records of the name and address of any child looked after on the premises;

6 requiring records to be kept of and notification of any changes in respect of persons who assist in looking after children and any person who lives or is likely at any time to be living at the premises.

If justified registration may be refused where a person is unfit or where the day care provided is *seriously inadequate* (having regard to the children's needs; particularly religious persuasion, racial origin and cultural and linguistic background).

The Department of Health and the Welsh office maintain in the 1992 Report that local authorities:

'... must strike the right balance between ensuring standards and encouraging the development of provision. There is a presumption under the legislation that registration should be granted unless the local authority has good reason not to register. Authorities ... should not apply the Department's guidance overrigidly or set standards higher than those recommended by the Department without good reason.'

The well publicised case concerning an appeal on 8 July 1993 in the Magistrates Court against The London Borough of Sutton's refusal to grant registration to a particular child minder, however, illustrates a problem here in the wording of the original guidance. Taking litigation against inaction is rendered difficult when many of the requirements are phrased as 'should' rather than 'must'. Thus they were thought (according to reporting in the media) not to apply in many situations. This lack of clarity has been further weakened by circular LAC(93)1 when it states that the guidance does not consist of legal requirements, rather it consists of 'factors to be considered and points of reference'. At the time of writing, it remains to be seen how the Sutton case is resolved in an appeal to the High Court.

Whilst the Department is confident that the circular will now assist local authorities to adopt a more constructive approach to regulation, changes have now been placed on top of the pre-existing guidance. As a result, the legal framework can no longer be said to be 'cut and dried'. Implementation presumes philosophy and at street level, aims that were said to have become skewed have now undergone a further twist. Presumptions under the legislation were, and still are, unclear.

The presumption has to be that the new guidance should supersede a major part of the old. This is technically not the case as the old guidance has not been withdrawn. This may have been the intention at the drafting stage of the circular in late 1992. The draft produced at that time was equally prescriptive and therefore seen unhelpful at the time and was not proceeded with.

Local needs and national concerns mixed together in variable quantities are a murky brew. Variations between different local authorities have been a particular feature of the public and private parts of the national system (Moss 1991). Levels of financial support given by local authorities to playgroups and resources allocated to the registration, supervision and support of public services have considerable variations (Statham et al 1990) Moss attributes these differences to 'a reluctance of successive Governments to set and enforce either national targets for levels of provision or ... national standards for supervision or support.' Reported practice (Elfer and Beasley 1991) under the old 1948 Act illustrates the portent where such historical problems may re-emerge:

'... (non-tangible) grounds must be properly underpinned by clear criteria, professional judgment and a fair assessment process to avoid over subjective and unreasonable judgments about adequacy of care.'

The history of promoting laissez-faire rather than standards and clear criteria (that it is here argued has now undergone a new and fresh chapter) was illustrated historically by the words of John Patten in 1983 when he was minister at the Department of Health, 'the level of childcare provision is a matter for local authorities to consider in the light of circumstances prevailing in their area'.

Costs are a primary factor in the question of standards and local variations in provision. According to Moss (1991) staff pay, conditions and training opportunities, adult, child ratios and standards of accommodation and equipment all have their price tag and there are considerable regional variations in cost:

'Costs in London are particularly high. Two non-profit nurseries in central London ... both charge over £100 per week' (Moss 1991).

Property costs appear however to be the most significant element in the financial equation here. A 1989 report on providing day care in a 24 place nursery in The Isle of Dogs gave the figure of £214 per week per child (mostly rent and rates). Staff costs amounted to 41% (Peat Marwick McLintock 1989).

'At the other extreme two nurseries in a shire county ... both of which only take children from 2 upwards ... charge £50 per week ... research evidence ... suggests that quality is influenced by conditions that involve higher costs, for example staff ratios and training so that some association between quality and cost might be expected ... The costs (generally) quoted include little or no element for support, career development and other measures likely to improve performance ... (they) ... are for a basic service with minimal working conditions. Even so, the costs to a parent are substantial and clearly put many options beyond the reach of many families.' (Moss 1991).

One example that has come to my notice, shows how demands by the Government put up costs. Requirements from other parts of the regulative system demands Tuberculosis tests for child minders, but the particular local Health Authority will not provide or pay for them. Thus the hapless prospective minder, if they are to register, must pay fees for tests from their GP. This procedure does not come cheap in poor communities. It is however derivative of policies of the same Department of Health that is now asking local authorities to reduce the costs of registration in day care.

According to discussion in the theory of the law of regulation in Cranston (1985), unless regulatory enforcement agencies regularly invoke the law, it will not be taken seriously. Enforcement has to be predictable or even the law-abiding will lack the incentive to adopt procedures which guarantee compliance with their legal obligations:

'However, an enforcement orientation does not necessarily mean strict enforcement in all (or even most) instances of non-compliance ... (as) ... the law would be brought into disrepute if formal legal proceedings were instituted for every trivial breach. The crucial point in control is that the law contemplates enforcement.'

It is now to be argued in most cases enforcement is now problematic as a result of the circular. It can always now be argued by an alert solicitor acting on behalf of a proprietor (unless children are absolutely in danger of abuse, in which case other provisions of the Act may apply) that local needs pertain. Following Cranston (1985) the law is no longer predictable and will be difficult to enforce. Thus it will probably not be taken seriously. The Department of Health has in effect brought the very law into disrepute by rendering enforcement impossible except in extreme cases. What legitimacy does the law have if it will hardly ever be actually enforced?

Local authorities who wish to impose conditions or refuse registration will now need to be very careful in putting together evidence for these cases. Crucial issues such as who are fit persons and what are safety standards may now have to be decided by precedents yet to be set in the courts. Taking the example of fit persons, the original guidance defined eight factors to be considered when fitness is to be assessed:

1 previous experience of looking after or working with young children or people with disabilities or the elderly;

2 qualification and/or training in a relevant field such as child care, early years education, health visiting, nursing or other caring activities;

3 ability to provide warm and consistent care; commitment and knowledge to treat all children as individuals and with equal concern;

4 knowledge of and attitude to multi-cultural issues and people of different racial origins;

5 physical health;

6 mental stability, integrity and flexibility;

7 known involvement in criminal cases involving abuse to children.

Circular LAC(93)1 however states that general overall fitness is pertinent rather than each individual factor being used to render a person unfit. The issue here is the overall quality of care that will be available to the children. This presumably means in practice that one authority's interpretation will be different from that of another until contested cases determine how the mix of factors, their respective importance and their bearing upon these principles of the circular actually determines the decision. This is the proverbial lawyer's field day! It is even more of a field day when all cases have to be heard in the courts rather than through mechanisms such as tribunals.

The circular seeks to define:

'... common factors and general points of reference' in interpretations of the fitness or unfitness of premises, and the standards of staff/child ratios and space. As such the Department considers that they may be amongst the points of reference in litigation over the reasonableness of registration decisions. The problem of the circular is that 'neither singly nor taken together are (these) ... prescribed.'

In passing the buck to local registration authorities to make their own judgments on criteria for the overall fitness or unfitness of all applications for registration, the Department wishes to have both its cake and eat it! Reasonableness in law is a question of interpretation and so again it is, and will be, a lawyer's field day.

The question of furniture, equipment, toys, and the use of space, in the original guidance are now 'advisory, and should not be insisted upon in the registration concerning facilities which, in the more important respects, are fit for their purpose.' The needs and preferences of parents and local needs are now said to be of more importance than overall standards.

My reading of the original guidance (DoH 1991) is that these items were generally prescriptive in tone rather than advisory. The word most generally used is 'should' (eg *should* hold relevant qualifications, *should* be qualified in child care, *should* take into account points listed concerning aspects of premises and space). Words like '*may* be taken into account' do not figure. In fairness to Circular LAC(93) the guidance was not expressed through mandatory words like *must*. Problems in questionable drafting that are emerging in cases like that in Sutton Magistrates Court are now, however, with the advent of circular LAC(93)1 further compounded.

Even in the question of ratios, the Department had made clear in the original guidance (DoH, 1991) their expectations that ratios higher than the prescribed norm were to be expected in some instances 'if not all the staff are qualified or sufficiently trained, if there are young babies (under 12 months) who need constant attention'. Thus it is to be expected that in some cases some authorities would apply ratios above the norm.

I would suggest that for political reasons the goal posts have now been moved. 'Reinterpretation' rather than a clear restatement of purpose and a firm redefining of guidance does not solve the dilemmas of the registration officer.

The variable, local prescription for interpretation of guidance made under the same overall statute is unhelpful, and is unlike most other areas of guidance under the Act. For example 'Working Together' (Home Office) et al, 1991) is to be followed quite slavishly unless criticism is to follow. As witness the tenor of many child abuse enquiries. Guidance in child protection is largely immutable. The preface to Working Together makes this clear, as although it 'does not have the full force of statute, (it) ... should be complied with unless local circumstances indicate exceptional reasons which justify a variation' (p iii). On the other hand, according to Circular LAC(93)1, guidance in day care means that 'Local needs should ... be respected.' Public pressures in child protection demand firm and absolute guidance that is close to being regulations. In day care public pressure demands in contrast a high degree of 'flexibility'. Guidance here according to Circular LAC(93)1 is now no more than a means to 'draw attention to factors that should be considered and points of reference'.

A market philosophy

Nationally, tinkering with markets rather than re-establishing clarity in standards and purpose may be said to derive from political and legal expediency. The rationale for intervention should be that the benefit (the welfare of the child) outweighs the costs (restriction upon the number of places locally and nationally available). Intervention is based entirely upon the shortcomings of the market (ie that it would otherwise exploit working mothers by providing day care facilities that may be substandard). Regulation will inevitably reduce numbers if they are to have any meaning. Markets express the relationship between price, costs and supply. Intervention through regulation will automatically alter this equation.

Moss (1991 p 84) maintains that:

> 'The Government want to see the market provide diversity, choice and good quality ... The clear objective ... is to encourage a market in under fives' services, paid for by parents (sometimes with the support of employers) and only diluted by a limited amount of state nursery education and very small quantities of public day care for children "in need" ... issues of access, equality, and segregation receive no attention ... childminding has (also) received official support ... (because of) ... low cost and flexibility.'

It could be argued that if the market were perfect in protecting the welfare of the child, demand for quality child care would automatically insist upon a quality product. As this is patently not the case in the evidence we have explored, the rationale and basis of that intervention should be examined.

The original goals of the government it may be argued were unclear. The welfare of the child is the main thrust of the Children Act and is said to be paramount. This rests uneasily, however, with a view expounded by the circular that day care should be expanded without putting more resources into the area. The question here is one actually raised within the circular, ie what is an acceptable standard?

The level of market equilibrium will be determined by the scope of intervention. The illusion of action under the 1948 Act already referred to (Freeman 1992) may be contrasted with actual action under the structures and philosophies of the Children Act in the early days of implementation. For the rest of the 1990s economic restraint is now a clear factor that is dictating compromise and lowering of standards.

It is in effect argued by the Government that efficiency is to be achieved by an expansion of day care provision that has no impact upon the treasury purse. The reality however is a methodology dictated by the economy of lower standards and by changingly fluid definitions of effectiveness.

Conclusions

The potential of the 1989 Children Act to enable day care provision of quality has been lost. The Department has acted as a dentist extracting the teeth of the registration officer leaving them powerless to insist upon standards. The under-regulation that denoted the ineffectiveness of the old 1948 Act has now re-emerged.

If the previous standards in the guidance were being over interpreted a restatement would be in order. 'Reinterpretation' merely constitutes a legal fudge in a territory marked out by economic and political expediency. What is now left is the worst of all worlds: lower standards, lack of clarity in the law, and a service that can develop only in terms of numbers of places and economy, rather than overall quality and effectiveness.

Bibliography and References

Cohen, B	'Caring for Children' The 1990 Report, Family Policy Studies Centre/Scottish Child and Family Alliance
Cranston, R	*Legal Foundations of the Welfare State* (1985) Weidenfield and Nicolson
Deech, R	Letter, *The Independent* (1991) 25 January
Dept of Health & Welsh Office	'The Children Act Report' (1992) Cm 2144 HMSO
Department of Health	'The Children Act 1989 Guidance and Regulations' (1991) Family Support, Day Care and Educational Provision for Young Children Vol 2 HMSO
Department of Health	The Children Act and Day Care for Young Children: Registration (1993) Circular LAC(93) 1 January Department of Health
Elfer, P Beasley, G	Registration of Childminding and Day Care; Using the 'law to improve standards' (1991) Department of Health HMSO
Freeman, MDA	'Children their Families and the Law, Working with the Children Act' (1992) MacMillan
Grice, E	'Mind Your Toys, The Inspectors Are Here' *Daily Telegraph* (1992) 29 October
Home Office, Dept of Health, Dept of Education & Science	'Working Together, A Guide to Arrangements for Inter Agency Co-operation for the Protection of Children Abuse' (1991) HMSO
Leader	*Independent* (1991) 23 September
Jones, J	'The UK has no National Strategy in Child Care, Unlike Denmark Where It Is a Major Issue' *The Independent* (1991) 23 September
Melhuish, E	'Research in Day Care in Britain' (1991) in Moss, P and Melhuish, E *Current Issues in Day Care for Young Children* DoH, HMSO
Moss, P	'Day Care Policy and Provision in Britain' (1991) in Moss, P and Melhuish, E *Current Issues in Day Care for Young Children* DoH, HMSO

Peat Marwick McLintock   'Childcare in Docklands: Making it Happen' (1989) Report to the London Docklands Corporation. Quoted in Moss (1991)

Pugh, G   'Services for Under Fives Developing a Co-ordinated Approach' (1988) National Children's Bureau London.

Statham, J, Lloyd, E, Moss, P, Melhuish, E, Owen, C   'Playgroups in a Changing World' (1990) London HMSO

Department of Health   'Voluntary Organisations Liaison Council for Under Fives' (1993) New Circular on Day Care, Children Act News

Chapter 8

Prohibited Steps Orders and the Protection of Children

Lindsey Mendoza
Anglia Polytechnic University

Introduction

One of the objectives of the Law Commission (Law Comm 172 1988) wished to achieve when suggesting reforms to the law relating to children was to reduce the necessity to resort to wardship both in the spheres of public and private law. Two new orders were created within s 8 of the Children Act 1989 - the prohibited steps order and the specific issues order. It was hoped that these two orders would incorporate into the statutory code some of the better features of the wardship jurisdiction.

Statutory definition of a Prohibited Steps Order

'Any order that no step which could be taken by a parent in meeting his parental responsibility for a child and which is of a kind specified in the order shall be taken by any person without the consent of the court.'(s 8(1) Children Act 1989).

Persons entitled to apply without leave of the court

The category of people who do not need leave of the court is contained within s 10(4) of the Act which says as follows:

'The following persons are entitled to apply to the court for any s 8 order with respect to a child.

(a) any parent or guardian of the child.

(b) any person in whose favour a residence order is in force with respect to the child.

It should be noted that a wider group of people under s 10(5) are entitled without leave to apply for a residence or contact order.

Persons entitled to apply with leave of the court

Under s 10(8) leave may be granted to the child themselves:

'Where the person applying for leave to make an application for a s 8 order is the child concerned, the court may only grant leave if it is satisfied that he has sufficient understanding to make the proposed application.'

Other people requiring leave to apply must satisfy the criteria laid down in s 10(9) of the Act:

' the court shall have particular regard to:

(a)   the nature of the proposed application for the s 8 order

(b)   the applicant's connection with the child

(c)   any risk there might be of the proposed application disrupting the child's life to such an extent that he would be harmedby it; and

(d)   where the child is being looked after by the Local Authority:

      (i)   the Authority's plans for the child's future; and

      (ii)   the wishes and feelings of the child's parents

The case of *Re M (Prohibited Steps Order: Application for Leave)* (1993)[1] dealt with two issues:

1   The status of a guardian *ad litem* as applicant;

2   Should an application for leave be heard *ex parte*.

The Local Authority as applicant

As a result of s 9(1) the Local Authority may only apply for a prohibited steps order if the child is not the subject of a care order. Section 9(1) states that:

'No court shall make any s 8 order other than a residence order with respect to a child who is in the care of the Local Authority.'

Another provision of the Act which is indirectly relevant to Local Authorities and their ability to apply for prohibited steps orders is s 9(2) which states that 'No application may be made by a Local Authority for a residence order or a contact order and no court shall make an order in favour of a Local Authority.'

Other relevant statutory provisions

Section 91(10):

'A s 8 order shall if it would otherwise still be in force, cease to have effect when the child reaches the age of 16, unless it is to have effect by virtue of s 9(6).' (Where there are exceptional circumstances.)

1   [1993] 1 FLR 275.

Section 9(5) contains a very important provision which is frequently referred to in the cases on prohibited steps orders. It states:

'No court shall exercise its jurisdiction to make a specific issues order or a prohibited steps order:

(a)   with a view to achieving a result which could be achieved by making a residence or contact order; or

(b)   in any way which is denied by the High Court by s 100(2) in the exercise of its inherent jurisdiction withrespect to children.'

The issue of parental responsibility

Does the respondent to an application for a prohibited steps order have to have parental responsibility for the child concerned? It is necessary to look again at the wording of s 8(1) and the definition of a prohibited steps order:

'... an order that no steps which could be taken by a parent in meeting his parental responsibility for a child and which is of a kind specified in the order shall be taken by any person without the consent of the court.'

It is clear from the wording that a prohibited steps order can be used to prevent people other than those with parental responsibility from doing something which could be classified as an aspect of parental responsibility.

An obvious example of where this might be necessary would be to prevent an unmarried father (who would not have parental responsibility unless he had acquired it) from removing his children from the country without the knowledge and consent of the mother.

Two cases illustrate that the category of 'any person' goes even wider. In *S v C* (1992)[2] a mother obtained (*inter alia*) a prohibited steps order against her child's grandmother preventing her from removing the child from her care. Price[3] describes a case which was heard at Wandsworth County Court. A mother and her boyfriend (who was not the father of her children) parted and the boyfriend moved out but continued to harass the mother and children outside the children's school and tried to interfere with their education by talking to their teachers. An injunction under the Domestic Violence and Matrimonial Proceedings Act 1976 was no longer appropriate nor was an action in assault and trespass. The mother applied for a residence order and a prohibited steps order to prevent the boyfriend removing the children from her care, attending at her home and the school, having any contact with them or molesting them.

---

2   [1992] 22 FL 134.
3   [1992] Fam Law 92.

Perhaps unfortunately there was not a substantive hearing as the boyfriend gave undertakings to the court but Price argues that under these circumstances a prohibited steps order would have been appropriate to deal with the interference in the children's education as clearly how a child is educated is an aspect of parental responsibility. The issue of the prevention of harassment is dealt with under item 4.

Prohibited steps orders and denial of contact

It is very common for the courts to be asked to deny contact between parent and child for a variety of reasons. Before the Act, if the court was of the opinion that access should be terminated or regulated in any way, the order was phrased in those terms. However since the Act, the prohibited steps order has been considered as an alternative. Indeed Lowe commented shortly after the Act came into force:

> 'Denial of contact must (now) take the form of a prohibited steps order since s 8. orders can only provide for positive contact ...'.[4]

This issue was raised in *Croydon LBC v A (No 1)* (1992)[5]. The Local Authority applied to the Family Proceedings Court for an interim care order in respect of a child who had sustained suspected non accidental injuries when with his father. The Bench declined to make the order and made two prohibited steps orders in the following terms:

1   The father was to have no contact with his children;

2   The parents were to have no contact with one another.

The Local Authority appealed against both prohibited steps orders. Not surprisingly the High Court allowed the appeal on the second point, as contact between parents is not an aspect of parental responsibility and therefore cannot be regulated by a prohibited steps order. The High Court also upheld the appeal on the first point due to the nature and facts of the case. Hollings J held that under the circumstances:

> 'The justices ... were plainly wrong to refuse to make an interim care order which would give more flexibility to the Local Authority ...'.

However, had the circumstances been less serious the prohibited steps order prohibiting contact between father and child may have been upheld. It should also be noted that the application in this case was made by the Local Authority rather than by an individual. Local Authorities face particular problems which will be examined under item 8.

---

4   [1992] Fam Law 67.
5   [1992] Fam Law 441.

The issue of denial of contact also came before the courts in *Nottingham County Council v P* (1993)[6]. The case is discussed more fully below but the case is of interest here due to the comments made by the President of the Family Division when the case reached the Court of Appeal (*The Times* 8 April 1993). The President addressed the issue of whether a contact order rather than a prohibited steps order could be made in a case where no contact is appropriate and he made the following comments:

'It had been submitted that a contact order implied a positive order and that an order which provided for no contact could not be construed as a contact order. The court did not accept that submission.

The sensible construction of the term 'contact order' included a situation where a court had to consider whether there should be any contact. Therefore an order that there should be no contact came within the general concept of contact and common sense required that it should fall within the definition of 'contact order' within s 8(1)'.

It would appear therefore that this recent interpretation of a contact order is wide enough to encompass an order for no contact thus rendering a prohibited steps order redundant under these circumstances. This may not be a decision which was envisaged and no doubt it will be referred to in future cases on this topic.

The injunctive quality of the Prohibited Steps Order and its regulation of certain aspects of parental responsibility

The Law Commission (para 4.15) discussed the MCR r 94(2) which stated that leave was required of the court if a custodial parent wished to take a child out of England and Wales (even for a short period such as a holiday). It was clearly felt that this rule was unrealistic but the Commission drew a distinction between a parent wishing to take his or her child on a holiday abroad and the parent wishing to reside abroad with the child. Concern was particularly expressed about the situation whereby one parent may wish to go abroad without the agreement of the other or even leave without telling the other parent. However now under s 13 of the Act if a residence order is in force, the parent in whose favour the order is made can now remove the child from the jurisdiction of the court for up to 28 days without applying for leave. This will obviously cover most holiday situations. For longer periods of absence the parent wishing to leave the country with the child must obtain the written consent of all persons with parental responsibility (which may not include an unmarried father) or obtain leave of the court.

---

6   [1993] Fam Law 222.

When discussing the situations in which a prohibited steps order may be appropriate, the Law Commission (para 4.20) stated:

'One example (of an appropriate use of a prohibited steps order) however, might be to ensure that the child is not removed from the United Kingdom, especially in the case where there is no residence order in force and the automatic prohibition (now under s 13(1)(b)) cannot apply.'

One of the first cases to use the prohibited steps order in this way was that of *Re D (A Minor) (Removal from the Jurisdiction)* (1992)[7]. This concerned a couple who were divorcing. Decree nisi had been pronounced and joint custody of the child awarded with care and control to the mother. The father applied *ex parte* for the following orders:

1   A specific issues order that the mother returned their young children from Turkey where she had gone presumably; to set up a new home as she had taken all her belongings with her.

2   A prohibited steps order preventing the mother from removing the child once returned.

The trial judge refused the application on the basis that the orders would be unenforceable as the mother was out of the jurisdiction.

On appeal Balcombe LJ said that there was nothing in the Act to preclude the court from making the two orders despite the fact that the mother had no assets in the country which could be sequestered.

In the case of *Re L (A Minor) (Removal from Jurisdiction)* (1993)[8] an unmarried mother and father separated. The mother stopped the father's contact with their child and married an Australian. The Family Proceedings Court made the following orders:

1   A residence order in favour of the mother;

2   A parental responsibility order in favour of the father;

3   A prohibited steps order in father's favour preventing the mother from removing child to Australia.

The mother appealed against the prohibited steps order. The father eventually withdrew his opposition to the appeal on the basis that:

1   The mother should encourage the child to write to the father;

2   She would keep him informed at all times of child's address either within the jurisdiction or abroad.

Thorpe J allowed the appeal by consent and made the comment that cases such as these should be dealt with by Family Division of the High Court as such cases 'often required a fine balance in their determination'.

---

7   [1992] Fam Law 243.
8   [1993] Fam Law 280.

It seems therefore that a prohibited steps order would have been an appropriate step, had the father not withdrawn his opposition, until the matter could be dealt with by the High Court.

Another recent case dealing with a similar issue was that of *Re R (A Minor)* (1993)[9]. A mother was engaged to a Spaniard and wanted to spend three months of 1993 in Tenerife with their three year old child to see how things worked out. The unmarried father of the child applied *ex parte* to the Family Proceedings Court for a prohibited steps order preventing the child's removal. This was granted. At a subsequent hearing the justices extended the order until March 1993. The mother appealed. On appeal to the High Court the order was not set aside. Thorpe J. stated that jurisdiction required the profoundest thought and the most careful planning before being launched.' He repeated that this type of case was more suited to Family Division of High Court. In the particular circumstances of this case he commented that a two week stay in Tenerife should have been sufficient for the mother to decide if she wanted to stay.

In *Re W B (Minors: Residence)* (1993)[10] a cohabiting couple split up and the mother indicated that she wished to move to the USA with the couple's children. The father applied to the Family Proceedings Court for a prohibited steps order to prevent the mother from removing he children from the jurisdiction. The justices made an interim order that the children live with the father until the mother returned from a preliminary visit to the USA. It was subsequently found that the man was not in fact the children's father. The justices then granted a residence order to the mother with weekend contact to the 'father'. The man then appealed on the basis that the justices had made no order restricting the removal of the children from the jurisdiction. The High Court allowed the appeal on this point. Thorpe J stated that the status quo should be preserved for the children by either a prohibited steps order or a residence order with conditions attached. In order not to fall foul of s 9(5) the latter would be more appropriate.

There is no express provision in the Children Act for the making of an *ex parte* residence order. This had been a cause of some concern as it was felt by practitioners and academics alike that this represented a potentially serious omission in the Act notwithstanding the fact that by its very nature the prohibited steps order was an appropriate order to apply for *ex parte*. However in the case of *Re B (A Minor: Residence Order)* (1992)[11] a father applied *ex parte* for a prohibited steps order for the return of an abducted child and for an interim residence order in respect of the children who were still living with him. The judge refused the application on the grounds that he had no jurisdiction to deal with the abduction or make an *ex parte* residence order.

9   [1993] Fam Law 312.
10 [1993] Fam Law 395.
11 [1992] Fam Law 228.

The father appealed and the Court of Appeal allowed the appeal. They granted an interim residence order in respect of all the children with directions that the abducted child be returned immediately to the father and the remaining children remain in his care until the inter parties hearing. Butler Sloss LJ stated that *ex parte* residence orders could be used in exceptional circumstances.

Although this case is very important for its decision on the use of *ex parte* residence orders its case illustrates that although the father initially applied for a prohibited steps order for the return of the abducted child a residence order with conditions attached was made due to the limitations imposed by s 9(5) of the Act.

Changing a child's surname is one aspect of parental responsibility that has always been regarded as a major step in the child's life. The situation frequently occurs whereby a parent, usually the mother, remarries or takes another partner and wants the child to take her new husband or partner's surname. The courts have been reluctant in these situations for children to lose this vital link with their natural parent, particularly where parent and child are still in contact. The case of *Re L (A Minor)* (1993)[12] illustrates the role a prohibited steps order may play in these difficult situations. A couple lived together and a child was born although by the time she was born the couple were living apart. There was a brief four month reconciliation when the child was two months old. It had been agreed between the parents that the child would have the father's surname and registration took place accordingly. After the father had left again the mother executed a Statutory Declaration (unknown to the father) changing the child's surname to that of the mother. Problems also arose in respect of contact between the child and the father due to the mother's opposition. Approximately one year after the relationship broke down the issues of contact and the child's name came before the County Court. The Judge made an initial order for supervised contact and a prohibited steps order prohibiting the child from being known by any name but the father's name and directing the mother to make a further statutory declaration to that effect. The mother appealed but the Court of Appeal upheld the prohibited steps order and stressed the importance of continuing links with the father.

Clearly here the prohibited steps order was being used as a form of mandatory injunction rather than to prevent an aspect of parental responsibility taking place. It may have been equally appropriate to have used a specific issues order in these circumstances. In the case of *Re G (A Minor)* (1993)[13] the Court of Appeal dismissed an appeal by a mother for a prohibited steps order to prevent a father sending their child to a boarding school. Again

---

12   [1993] (unreported)
13   [1993] (unreported).

where the issue of a child's education is concerned a specific issues order will also be an appropriate order to consider. Indeed in many cases it is probably more appropriate that a prohibited steps order is made.

The issue of domestic violence

Occasionally where there is family breakdown there will be the issue of domestic violence to address. This may be violence against a parent or a child or both. The domestic violence legislation may not always be appropriate, particularly if the parties are no longer living together. Can prohibited steps orders be of any use in these situations? The answer is negative in almost every case as violence and harassment are not aspects of parental responsibility which can be regulated by a prohibited steps order. The point is well documented by Price (*ante*) when he says:

> 'Surely Parliament did not intend contact to include molestation and assault. These are not steps one would expect (a parent) to take in meeting his parental responsibility. It seems there is no power in Part 2 of the Act to protect children - only to regulate what would otherwise be the lawful exercise of parental responsibility.'

Three cases have addressed this issue:

In the case of *S v C* (*ante*) a mother took proceedings against her child's grandmother to restrain her from:

1   Assaulting her (the mother); and

2   Removing her child from her care.

The County Court granted a non-molestation injunction under s 38 County Courts Act 1984 ancillary to her application for a prohibited steps order.

The case of *J&W* (1992)[14] concerned the issue of harassment of a family. A mother wanted an injunction against the unmarried father of her twins. The couple now lived apart. There had been one serious violent incident against the mother but the father had continued to harass the mother (stopping short of actual violence). An application for a prohibited steps order was made although the solicitors for the mother had doubts as to whether a prohibited steps order was appropriate to protect the mother. The case was heard by the Family Proceedings Court as the LAB had refused legal aid for the case to be heard in the county court.

The Bench refused to hear case on the basis that:

1   A prohibited steps order cannot protect an adult ill-treatment of child;

---

14   [1992] Legal Action 21.

2   A prohibited steps order relates to an aspect of parental
       responsibility which does not cover the ill-treatment of children.

The case was then heard at the Principal Registry of the Family Division.
On this occasion the mother, as advised by counsel, applied for a residence
order in respect of the children so that a non molestation injunction could be
granted ancillary to the residence order. The orders were granted. The District
Judge did not extend the injunctions to protect the children as in this case it
was unnecessary, but he commented that the injunction could have covered
the children had it been necessary. Thus the matter was dealt with by way of a
residence order with an ancillary injunction rather than by way of a prohibited
steps order as harassment is not an aspect of parental responsibility!

The case of *M v M* (1992)[15] is a further illustration of the courts having to
deal with the issues of domestic violence and the children's future at the same
time. The case concerned a married couple. The husband was a violent man
and as a result of this, over a period of time, the wife became ill and was
admitted to a psychiatric hospital suffering from stress and psychosis. There
were two children of the family aged seven and eight. Two days after the
mother was discharged the father applied and was granted an *ex parte* interim
residence order in respect of the children and a prohibited steps order
preventing the mother from removing the children from the father's care. The
mother was unaware of the father's application and made her own application
ex parte for an ouster order against the father.

Eventually the two matters were heard together in the County Court and the
District Judge made the following two prohibited steps orders:

1   Forbidding the father from assaulting the mother;

2   Forbidding the father's mother and sister from living in or
       entering the matrimonial home. (They had moved in while the
       mother was in hospital.)

The mother appealed against these two orders on the following grounds:

1   The judge had erred in law by making prohibited steps orders in
       the above terms as assault was not an aspect of parental
       responsibility. She argued that the judge should have made
       orders under s 38 and s 39 of the County Courts Act 1984
       ancillary to an order regulating the father's contact with the
       children;

2   The judge had wrongly exercised his discretion by failing to
       grant an exclusion order against the mother-in-law and sister-in-
       law.

She argued that a prohibited steps order can only prevent actions which a
parent would take in meeting his parental responsibility. She further argued

---

15   [1992] 2 FLR 303.

that the exclusion of the mother-in-law and the sister-in-law could have been achieved by way of injunctions ancillary to the father's contact order. The High Court granted the mother's appeal and substituted two new orders:

1   Forbidding the husband from assaulting the wife; and

2   Restraining the mother and sister in law from entering the matrimonial home and interfering with the mother's exercise of her parental responsibility. The court held that prohibited steps orders were inappropriate here and that injunctions can be sought ancillary to s 8 orders- in this case ancillary to the contact order in favour of the father.

The Local Authority and Prohibited Steps Orders

A Local Authority can apply for a prohibited steps order but subject to the restrictions imposed by s 9(1) (*ante*). There are therefore only going to be a limited number of circumstances in which the Local Authority will be able to apply for such an order. Reference has already been made to the case of *Nottinghamshire County Council v P (ante)*. This concerned the alleged sexual abuse by a father against his daughters. The two younger daughters were considered by the Local Authority to still be at risk while the father remained in the same household. This case illustrates that not only are Local Authorities constrained by s 9(1) of the Act but by s 9(2) and s 9(5) as well. The Local Authority were initially granted a prohibited steps by the Family Proceedings Court requiring the father to leave the family home and not return. On appeal to the High Court Ward J held that by virtue of s 9(2) and s 9(5) the prohibited steps order could not stand. There was an existing application by the father for a residence order which of course had not been continued. Ward J therefore used his jurisdiction under s 10(1) to make a residence order in favour of the mother with a condition attached that the father be excluded from the home.

The matter then came before the Court of Appeal who dismissed the orders made by the High Court. The President of the Family Division stated that 'The judge had adopted an artificial course and said that he was driven to take some steps in order to protect the children.' The President acknowledged that by dismissing the orders he had left the children with no protection. He went on to criticise the Local Authority for not commencing care proceedings bearing in mind the circumstances of the case.

It is easy to see why care proceedings in this case may have been appropriate but there will be cases where the use of care proceedings is too draconian a remedy and a prohibited steps order would be the preferred option of the Local Authority. Once again they may well find themselves in the position of being unable to adopt this course of action. Indeed following the

High Court decision in the Nottinghamshire case, Lowe[16] made the following observation:

'As Ward J acknowledged, his ruling that a court cannot upon application by a Local Authority make a prohibited steps order ... (ordering) that a father should leave and not return to the household and that his children should have no further contact with him is bound to cause disquiet among the many Local Authorities which seek to use s 8. rather than invoking the case and supervision jurisdiction.'

It is unfortunate that the Local Authorities are going to be hampered in this way, bearing in mind the non-interventionist philosophy behind the Act, and the restrictions now imposed on Local Authorities by s 100 of the Act. It will be recalled that the Law Commission (*ante*) hoped that prohibited steps orders and specific issues orders would alleviate the need for individuals and Local Authorities to resort to Wardship or to use the inherent jurisdiction of the High Court.

Conclusion

Clearly the interpretation of s 8 has had 'teething troubles' particularly in respect of the scope and limitations of the prohibited steps order. However, some guidelines are now emerging, over how best to utilise these orders.

Prohibited steps orders can play a valuable role in regulating certain aspects of parental responsibility such as removing children from the country of changing their surname. However, Judges are conscious of the restrictions placed upon them by s 9(5) and in appropriate cases other orders such as residence orders are made with appropriate conditions attached.

It is also now clear that anyone carrying out an aspect of parental responsibility in an inappropriate manner can be a respondent to a prohibited steps order, even if they themselves do not have parental responsibility. Equally it is clear that a prohibited steps order is not appropriate in preventing assault either on children or their parents, as assault and molestation are not aspects of parental responsibility. The cases dealing with these issues illustrate that a more appropriate step is to order an injunction ancillary to a residence or contact order, whether it be the parent or child being assaulted, so that the parent is left free to carry out all aspects of parental responsibility free from interference by the perpetrator of the violence.

---

16   [1993] Fam Law 222.

Local Authorities usage of prohibited steps orders may need to be re-examined with a view to making it easier for them to use such orders, together with a specific issues orders, where children are not in care and care proceedings are inappropriate. Clearly the Law Commission did not envisage prohibited steps being used very frequently but is equally clear that prohibited steps orders do have an important role to play in child protection.

Chapter 9

The Implementation of the Requirements of the Children Act 1989 in Respect of Day Care Services

Margaret Ford Bolton, Business School BIHE
Nell Wood, Inspection Unit Social Service
Bolton Metropolitan Borough Councill

This paper is one approach to the requirements of the Act; a desire to implement 'good practice' and create a standardised approach to policy and procedure documentation and to address the implications for Inspection Units.

Introduction

Introducing the legislation in the House of Lords, the Lord Chancellor said. 'The Children Bill represents the most comprehensive and far reaching reform of child law which has come before Parliament in living memory'. The registration, inspection and general control of Children's facilities is governed by the provisions of the Children Act 1989 Part X.

The key messages in the Act are: the *child* is the most important person in our public and private lives: the needs of the *child* are paramount. The Act states the minimum standard of day care for young children in a multi-cultural and multi-racial society in partnership with parents. A major thrust is to promote inter-agency co-operation with the Courts and Social Services most centrally involved. However, liaison is mandatory in some areas eg day care, education supervision orders.

In order to introduce a system to implement the Act, Bolton Metropolitan Borough Council set up policy and procedures to introduce and maintain 'good practice'.

The methodology used, the implications and evaluation will now be discussed.

Background

Local Authorities have been registering and inspecting private and voluntary residential homes for frail old people and other vulnerable groups for a long time. Additional responsibilities have clearly been introduced by legislation. 'Children in the Public Care' (a review of Residential Child Care Part 1 HMSO 1991 by Sir William Utting) was commissioned by the Secretary of State following the publication of the 'Pindown Experience' Report

(Staffordshire County Council 1991) which examined the broader context to the management and control of Children's Homes. That context included: the collapse in the number of residents during the last decade, an associated loss of purpose and direction, deficiencies in policy management, a largely unqualified and inexperienced staff and problems of control in homes.

The Children Act came into force on the 14 October 1991. It reflects a convergence of values about children as individuals in their own right; citizens enjoying legal protection; the parents of tomorrow's children and the future of our society.

Under the Community Care Implementation, Inspection Units LAC(90)13, directions were made by the Secretary of State concerning the setting up of Inspection Units and other related matters. Local Authorities were required to set up Inspection Units to inspect residential homes in the public, private and voluntary sectors by 1 April 1991 and to establish advisory committees in support of this activity.

The Inspection Units became the responsible body to register and inspect private, voluntary and local authority residential homes (Residential Homes Act 1984) as well as all child care facilities including residential (Children Act 1989).

Method of approach

Local Authorities can be direct providers of day care alongside other direct providers in the private and voluntary sectors but they also have responsibilities to these sectors: the duty to regulate standards (Part X); the duty to facilitate the provision of day care (s 17); the power to provide training, advice, guidance and counselling to anyone caring for children whilst in day care (s 18).

In order to implement these requirements an information pack was designed. The collation of all the information within the document was made by the use of a Forcefield analysis and careful timescales were adhered to.

The Forcefield analysis is a way of listing each area of importance in implementing the policy and procedure documentation by considering the major driving forces and the main restraining forces which would affect it. Major areas for consideration were research; planning; consultation; analysis; producing the draft document; evaluation; second round of consultation and implementation (for an example of the process see Table 1). A realistic timescale for implementation was assessed (for example see Table 2). The interaction between the driving and restraining forces are self explanatory and serve to highlight the legislation or just parts of it (for a list of interest groups to be consulted see Table 3).

Implications for Inspection Units

The implications are wide ranging. Our example of the process of setting up a policy and procedure document and an information pack for Day Care for young children is an example of the workload placed on Inspection Units to implement the requirements of the Children Act 1989; Community Care Act 1990; Registered Homes (Amendment) Act 1991. There are also the requirements to produce policy and procedures to set up and maintain standards of practice; to involve and consult interested parties and to have both an advisory and regulatory function.

The above are obvious implications for Inspection Units. However, there are other subtle and less easily evaluated issues which will need attention in the near future.

Discussion

In 1991, after consultation, the Government arranged for Local Authorities to inspect the residential homes they run themselves so that the same standards would apply to them as to private and voluntary homes. It is not in dispute that inspection units in this wider role have done much good work (Inspecting Social Services 1992 - foreword by the Secretary of state for Health).

It was also advised that Inspection Units must be at 'arms length' from Local Authority service providers (The Griffiths Report). But, the units are to date under the direction of the Director of Social Services.

This situation must create a dichotomy. Authorities are also providers of Social Services. Until 1991, they were under no obligation to inspect their own residential homes for adults.

Since the Government has required them to inspect their own homes for adults from the same Inspection Units which inspect those in the independent sectors; they also use these units to inspect their own Children's residential homes.

Inspectors would seem to be in a compromising situation. Their role is clearly defined but this has created pressures (albeit subtle ones). Workloads are high; timescales are tight. Status and career positions in the units have in some circumstances led to disappointment. Legislation and directions on the role and framework of the Inspection Units do in essence create a highly stressful working environment. The inspectors must implement the legislation. They must be (and are) professional in approach and yet the difficulties in this do exist. Social Services Departments are the employer; they provide facilities, premises etc and they pay the salaries. The inspectors are called upon to be regulators of their own Local Authority as a provider.

Other issues probably fit within a political perception. Units ought not to be a means of 'pushing' particular local authority policy nor should the Inspection Unit advice be ignored when it comes to in-house facilities.

Another area of tension (whether real or imaginary) is in the requirement and desire to be objective and professional while working within the registration and regulatory framework. Inspection units can be perceived by providers in a variety of ways; as a friend or foe; as a threat; as a pressure point to gain extra resources.

There is a perception in the independent sector that there may be bias towards the local authority as provider. Inspectors need to demonstrate even-handedness and be seen to use and maintain the same methodology and standards across both sectors.

The need for a totally independent inspectorate would seem to be one way forward both in terms of provider perceptions (both local authority and independent) and as a means of redefining the status and role of inspectors in order to alleviate some of the stress and tensions currently experienced by them.

The way forward

The recent reform of community care for adults and of children's services include important changes which ought to improve standards and give individual users and their carers better ways of influencing the services they receive within available resources. These include clear and efficient systems of management and reinforced by an effective complaints process and by objective and independent inspections (Inspecting Social Services Department of Health 1992).

In addition, The Citizen's Charter described the role of public service inspectorates. The Charter emphasised the value that lay people can bring to inspections; the importance of openness in handling and responding to inspection reports and the need for independence between those who carry out inspections and those responsible for managing the services being assessed. At present responsibility for inspecting Social Services lies with both local and central government.

The Shire counties, Metropolitan districts and London boroughs are currently the statutory registration bodies for private and voluntary residential homes for adults and of private residential homes for children and young people. They also register day care for young children and childminders. Authorities inspect all these facilities before giving the registration that is mandatory before these services can be offered to the public. They also inspect the welfare arrangements for children in independent boarding schools. All this work is carried on by Inspection Units.

The Government intends to implement a phased development programme which builds on what has already been achieved. This programme will include the enhancement of the independence of inspectors.

The independence of Inspection Units from the services they inspect is essential and the Government has recognised that the dual responsibility placed on local authorities could generate a conflict of roles.

The Government has no doubt that the regulatory role with regard to Social Services which is placed on local authorities by legislation should be the responsibility of their Social Services Committees. It does consider that the important objective of Inspection Unit independence would be more clearly defined if the reporting line at officer level were to the Chief Executive and it is the intention that local authorities by next Autumn should plan with change in mind.

In 1995 progress will be reviewed and the Government will consider what further steps will be necessary to achieve the essential objectives of effectiveness and independence.

Bibliography and References

HMSO Publications   'Childminder's Non-Domestic Premises
                             71(1)(b)' The Children Act 1989 Part 10

National Children's Bureau   'Young Children in Group Daycare
                             Guidelines for Good Practice'

National Childminders'   'Setting the Standards - Guidelines on
Association   Good Practice in Registering Childminders'

National Children's Bureau   'Setting the Standards in the Care of
Early Childhood Unit   Young Children'

Pre-school Playgroup   Guidelines
Association

Department   'Inspecting Social Services'
of Health

HMSO   'Children in the Public Care' SS1
                             'Community Care Implementation
                             Inspection Units' LAC(90)13
                             'Inspection of Community Homes'
                             LASC(92)14

Table 1
Force Field Analysis for Research
(Children Act 1989 – Implementation)

Research

DRIVING FORCE	RESTRAINING FORCE
Aims and objectives	Knowledge of legislation
Philosophy	Process of collating information
Responsibilities	Identification of named person
Values	Based on quality care
Training	Resource and time implications
Agencies involved (professional contributors)	Identify, consult, time
Agencies involved (providers of service)	Identify, consult, time
Department input	Time needed for return of information
Budget for implementation	To be identified by Deputy Director
Service delivery	Knowledge, resource, timescale
Who should perform task	Registration and Inspection Unit

Planning

DRIVING FORCE	RESTRAINING FORCE
Timescale	January 1992
Consultations	Cooperation and contribution
Administration time	Cost
Documentation	Collation of information
Printing information pack	Accuracy, physical production cost, timescale
Management of agency and politician feedback	Co-ordinating meetings Acceptance or alteration

Table 2
Time Management for Implementation Process

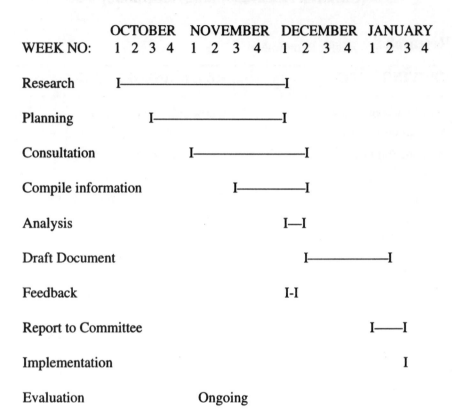

	OCTOBER	NOVEMBER	DECEMBER	JANUARY
WEEK NO:	1 2 3 4	1 2 3 4	1 2 3 4	1 2 3 4
Research	I————————————I			
Planning	I————————I			
Consultation	I————————I			
Compile information	I————————I			
Analysis	I—I			
Draft Document	I————————I			
Feedback	I-I			
Report to Committee	I———I			
Implementation	I			
Evaluation	Ongoing			

A deadline of Week 4 January 1992 was decided with initial research, planning and consultation beginning Week 1 October 1991. Six weeks were allowed for consultation interviews. (In fact more than 20 interviews were carried out with appropriate agencies, eg RSPCA.) Research was ongoing until December. Feedback to agencies had to be complete by Week 2 December 1991 to allow for documentation production and reporting to Social Services Committee. Implementation was to Schedule. The evaluation continues.

Table 3
List of Agencies Consulted in order to Produce Policy and Procedure Documentation and Information Pack

Environmental Health Department

Leisure Services

Finance Department (Social Services)

Planning Department

Community Education

Social Services Inspectorate

RSPCA

Health and Safety Executive

National Childminders' Association

Families Together, Social Services

Principal Officer, Children and Families Team

Greater Manchester County Fire Service

Education for Special Needs

Greater Manchester Police

Senior Relations Officer

Voluntary Organisation and Training

Road Safety Officer

Catering Manageress Bolton Social Services

Consultant Community Paediatrician

Pre-school Playgroup Association

Private Day Nursery Association

Note   A Forcefield Analysis was also produced for the consultation stage of implementation.